THE MARDLER'S COMPANION

Mardle. Can be used either as a verb, to gossip or chat, or as a noun, "we had a rare good ol' mardle, he and I".

Overleaf: *Furze-cutting on a Suffolk Common, by Peter Henry Emerson.*

THE
MARDLER'S
COMPANION

A dictionary of
East Anglian dialect

ROBERT MALSTER

MALTHOUSE PRESS, SUFFOLK 1999

Published by Malthouse Press, Suffolk,
17 Reade Road,
Holbrook,
Suffolk, IP9 2QL.

Cased ISBN 0 9522355 7 9
Limp ISBN 0 9522355 8 7

British Library Cataloguing-in-Publication Data

A catalogue record for this book is available from the British Library.

Designed by Robert Malster.
Typeset by John Walton.
Printed in Great Britain by
Wolsey Press, Ipswich.

Foreword

From the beginnings of its history the English language has developed an extraordinary range of varieties. These include a standard written, and later spoken, variety, a wealth of slang and colloquial expressions, numerous specialised terms relating to occupations and professions and, above all, a unique profusion of regional and social dialects. Regional speech maintains its distinctiveness today, notably in pronunciation or accent, but also in vocabulary, and to some extent in grammar.

While accent may identify the regional and/or social background of individual speakers, it is the words they use which often mark them out as coming from a specific area. Over the centuries each part of the country has inherited its own wordstock which has become a hall-mark of local identity. In the twentieth century, however, and especially during the past fifty years, the number and variety of regional dialect words have been subject to increasing erosion and change. The erosion is due to many factors, including major changes in our way of life, especially in the countryside, and to the impact of technology, the advent of universal education and the mass media, along with a much more mobile population.

These changes have not been uniform across the country, and are especially evident in urban centres where people from many different geographical and social origins mingle, leading to a certain ironing out of local distinctiveness. Even so, we can still recognise the differences in speech from one urban area to another. In many rural areas, despite techno-logical developments in agriculture and the consequent decline of the ancient handcrafted trades formerly common in many villages and small towns, regional dialects persist, not only among the older generation but also in the words and expressions in the everyday usage of many younger people. Because we are used to hearing such words, we may not realise that they are local, or that they are part of a wider range of terms which may also be known or used in other areas, but are not in the standard language.

In those parts of the country where the older lifestyles and ways of working have been in some respects slower to change, many regional dialects have remained comparatively conservative, retaining much of the old while gradually adopting the new. To some extent this has been true of parts of East Anglia, certainly until the 1950s. Notwithstanding the modernisation in agriculture and in social and domestic life evident throughout rural England, the casual visitor to parts of rural Norfolk and Suffolk today may well find that, as in other such areas, certain traditional patterns of life and work have persisted longer than in most urban centres. In consequence, the characteristic local accents and vocabulary often remain in active use. All the more reason, then, to put on record an account of the regional dialect words typical of the area, both in the past and within living memory.

It so happens that the speech of East Anglia has been a subject of enquiry since the seventeenth century. The published glossaries, collections and accounts of the dialect there-fore provide unusually full and detailed information for tracing its history and for under-taking comparative studies of the vocabulary over an unusually lengthy timespan. The author of *The Mardler's Companion* has taken full advantage of this long historical record. He has gathered together a fascinating list of East Anglian dialect words and expressions, culled from the various dictionaries and glossaries and from more than fifty years of personal observation. His interest in dialect was sparked off by a series of letters on "Broad Norfolk" published in the *Eastern Daily Press* shortly after the end of the second world war, a selection of which was published as a small booklet. With these as a starting point, he built up the substantial collection of material which makes up the present volume.

He shared his passion for dialect with his father, who was interested in Dutch and the Scandinavian languages. Together they researched and wrote an article entitled "A New Approach to Dialect" in which they investigated the foreign origins of dialect words and grammar. As the collection grew, the author added his own knowledge and memories of East Anglian dialect and then began the lengthy process of checking the terms in the *Oxford English Dictionary* and the available printed works on the subject to establish their origin, provenance and meaning.

In this highly accessible book the reader will discover a treasure hoard of local words and expressions, both familiar and unfamiliar. Many of the entries are accompanied by illuminating commentaries and helpful references to parallel examples in printed sources. From *alegar, argufy, dardledumdue, didapper* and *molgogger* to *pickcheese, tuttle, tye* and *ungain,* the local speech of East Anglia is presented in all its rich variety. Even more compelling, however, are the longer entries on aspects of language, rural life, and the previous writers on local dialect and history, along with the author's knowledgeable comments on local usage, often setting words and phrases in the full context of living speech, as witnessed over more than half a century of keen observation.

For everyone interested in English regional language, *The Mardler's Companion* is a most welcome compendium of East Anglian dialect past and present. For those who live in the area or who cherish its unique heritage, this handy new volume is essential reading.

J.D.A. Widdowson
National Centre for
English Cultural Tradition
University of Sheffield

Acknowledgments

The compilation of this dictionary is the outcome of an interest that was fanned into an enthusiasm by the publication first of a series of letters to the Eastern Daily Press and then of a little book called *Broad Norfolk* in 1949. My own copy soon grew by the addition of inter-leaves on which were pasted those letters that were not reprinted in the book, plus many later letters and articles.

That was just a beginning. Before long I was dipping into the Rev Robert Forby's *The Vocabulary of East Anglia* and Major Edward Moor's *Suffolk Words and Phrases*, both of which proved to be of absorbing interest. I acquired, too, a copy of the English Dialect Society publication of 1879 containing the Rev W.T. Spurdens' supplement to Forby, and in due time was introduced to other dialect publications. And like others I revelled in Sidney Grapes' occasional letters in the *Eastern Daily Press* telling of the life of the Boy John, Granfar and Arnt Agatha.

I do not think that it occurred to me in those days that I might have spoken dialect myself; my schoolteachers had done their best to ensure that I spoke "proper English", and I chided my mother for her double negatives. It was only when I spoke into a tape-recorder for the first time at a show at the Agricultural Hall in Norwich (now the headquarters of Anglia Television) that I discovered how strong was my accent, and only later that I realised how much of what I said came out in non-standard English.

In his introductory article in *Broad Norfolk* Eric Fowler, writing under his pseudonym of "Jonathan Mardle," expressed a hope that fifty years thence there might be a third edition — the first had been produced in 1893 as the result of a similar correspondence. Almost fifty years has passed, and perhaps this compilation, throwing its net a little wider, would meet with his approval.

It is therefore appropriate that I should first of all express my gratitude to Eric Fowler for having encouraged my interest half a century ago. Maybe, too, I should express thanks to the anonymous marshman who, during an encounter on the Hoveton to Horning road in the vicinity of Hoveton Little Broad, inquired in good Norfolk dialect if I could "lend him ten bob till the weather breaks".

Since then many people have helped me in my researches. Among them are Christine and David Cleveland, Maryan and Roy Fidler, Phil Gray, Derek and Mary Manning, Hector Moore and his wife Mary, Peter Northeast, Dr J.D.A. Widdowson, Director of the National Centre for English Cultural Tradition at the University of Sheffield, David Woodward, and of course my parents. I am also indebted to Mrs Ruth Serjeant, who suggested the title of this book. Many others have earned my thanks for their help and encouragement, not least Norman Scarfe for a generous contribution from the Scarfe Charitable Trust towards the cost of publication.

To them all, and to the many whose names I have forgotten, I express my thanks. If this book succeeds in its object, the credit should go to them; for the errors and omissions I must take the blame.

In *Broad Norfolk* Eric Fowler said that he felt he had chronicled another phase in the decline of local dialect but, like Charles II, it was an unconscionable time dying, and there should be no more rash prophecies about its extinction. Fifty years on one has real fears for the survival of the language of East Anglia; yet perhaps it would not be out of place to express a fervent hope, long may it reign!

A portrait of an East Anglian seafarer of early this century, typical of the men who manned the old pulling and sailing lifeboats.

Nelson's native tongue

Lord Nelson lay in the cockpit of his flagship, his spine shattered by a musket ball fired by a marksman from the mizzen-top of the *Redoubtable*. The agony of his fatal wound came and went; at times he drifted off into near-unconsciousness, at other times he was alert and sought news of the battle.

Eventually Thomas Masterman Hardy, his Flag Captain, came to him with the news he sought. Fourteen or fifteen of the enemy ships had surrendered. "That's well, but I bargained for twenty," Nelson replied. Then, feeling the swell rising under the battered *Victory*, he told Captain Hardy, "Anchor, Hardy, anchor!"

The battle was almost over, and so was his life. His men had fought well, and they deserved a respite, those who could enjoy it. Some lay not far from him, their groans and cries showing that for them there was no rest. In his last minutes Nelson lapsed into the vernacular that he had spoken since his boyhood in North Norfolk. "Do you anchor, Hardy!"

Some naval historians have been puzzled by this remark. Was it a question? Those who share Nelson's pride in his East Anglian upbringing know it was nothing of the kind. It was an order, or if not an order it was a piece of emphatic advice to a subordinate whom he counted as a friend. "Do you anchor, Hardy!"

*   *   *

Nelson was proud of his East Anglian upbringing, he was proud of his Norfolk accent, and he made no attempt to hide it. Many others, too, have not been ashamed to speak the language of their own region.

Our dialect goes back a long way. Read the Paston Letters and one recognises many of the turns of phrase and quirks of grammatical construction that have remained features of East Anglian speech up to the present.

Of course it has not always been acceptable to some people. It is curious to read in nineteenth-century books that many people who were considered educated made the "mistake" of speaking in dialect, using the double negative that is typical of the East Anglian manner of speech or the separable prefix that is regarded as "wrong" by the speaker of Received English.

To Lord Nelson his speech was no mistake.

Introduction

Our dialect has been under threat for a great many years, never more so than at the end of the twentieth century. The Rev Robert Forby, whose book *The Vocabulary of East Anglia* was published in 1830, warned that "it is in danger of perishing when village carpenters shall attend, as a part of their education, a course of lectures at a Mechanic's Institution", and others have expressed similar misgivings down the years since. Yet it has survived, until now.

When a year or two back the Government-appointed National Curriculum Council was said to be considering a purge on spoken dialect in schools some of those who protested at the suggestion confused dialect with local accents. The two are quite different things, for all that they normally go together.

Others saw dialect as no more than a use of strange words which were not common to the English spoken in other parts of Britain. It is far more than that, for dialect has its own grammatical structure, sometimes quite different from the "normal" grammar of the language as it used to be taught in schools.

What, then, is dialect? The *Oxford English Dictionary*, that arbiter of "proper" English, tells us that it is one of the subordinate forms or varieties of a language arising from local peculiarities of vocabulary, presentation and idiom. That definition makes it clear that dialect is much more than an ignorant variation on correct English.

One of the earliest writers on the East Anglian dialect, Major Edward Moor, remarked on the fact that many words commonly used in Suffolk at the beginning of the nineteenth century, and even then considered to be peculiar to the dialect, were to be found in Shakespeare's writing.

That strange comment that somebody knew "a hawk from a handsaw" that has puzzled generations of schoolboys studying Shakespeare is easily explained when one has a knowledge of the dialect. It is nothing to do with a tool for cutting wood; anyone native to Norfolk or Suffolk knows that the local name for a heron is a harnser. He who could not tell a hawk from a harnser was unable to distinguish between the hunter and its quarry, for the fashionable young gentleman was wont to fly his hawks against such prey.

This dialect word is no more than a contraction of the old word heronshaw, as used by Chaucer. In the Squire's Tale he writes "I wol nat tellen . . . of hir swannes nor of hir heronsewes".

It is no coincidence that we find so great a similarity between the dialect and the language of Chaucer and Shakespeare. Much that is found in the East Anglian dialect has survived from the time of Chaucer, and from earlier times. As George Ewart Evans points out in *Where Beards Wag All*, the continuity that the dialect shows with the earliest period of English literature is sufficient to dispose of the assertion made by educationists that it is not "proper English".

Ewart Evans went further, maintaining that it was not only in the language that one found this continuity with a distant past. Many of the structures of East Anglian society, its lore and its attitudes were derived from the early medieval period.

One who might be described as the father of oral history, Ewart Evans wrote of the East Anglian dialect not as a scholar who studied its nuances from an academic tower but as one who lived and worked with those who spoke it. He has left us all in his debt.

While some nineteenth-century writers such as the Rev F. Barham Zincke regarded dialect as an impoverished form of language, Ewart Evans was always keen to point to the richness of dialect speech, to the imagery employed by the dialect speaker. The much-heard modern expressions "sort of" and "ye know" were never resorted to by men and women of what he called "the prior culture". A good example of the imagery to which Ewart Evans referred was provided by a countryman (not an East Anglian) who in a radio programme on one of the battles of the First World War spoke of advancing men being cut down by German machine-guns "like sickled corn".

*   *   *

Dialect has been a source of interest to people for at least three hundred years. Sir Thomas Browne (1605–1682), the Norwich physician, was aware of the existence of a Norfolk dialect and was probably the first to make notes of its peculiarities. Then, at the beginning of the eighteenth century, a John Steele set down a list of provincial words, since preserved in the Bodleian Library at Oxford and made use of by more than one later collector. In the nineteenth century others set out to record "the vulgar tongue", and the publications resulting from their work have proved a rich mine for later researchers.

Dialect was already well established when Sir Thomas Browne's inquiring mind was leading him to note down strange local words at the same time that he collected his not-quite-understood scientific curiosities. It had originated in the speech of the Anglo-Saxons who settled in the region after the decline of Roman civilisation, and shows clear traces of having assimilated elements from other languages spoken by later invaders and settlers who came to the region from over the sea.

The men who buried their kings at Sutton Hoo, across the Deben from the town of Woodbridge, spoke a language that they had brought from the country of their origin, Sweden. Later settlers from the Netherlands introduced words and phrases from their native language, and other newcomers also added fresh elements to the rich vernacular speech. It has been pointed out by Peter Trudgill in *The Dialects of England* that in the twelfth century Norwich was a cosmopolitan city with substantial groups of people who spoke not only English but French, Danish, Dutch and the Jewish form of Spanish known as Ladino.

Most likely the variations found in dialect in different parts of East Anglia owe something to the men who settled in particular places. It would not be surprising if the dialect in the Flegg area to the north of Yarmouth showed more evidence of Scandinavian influence than that spoken in areas where Norse settlement was less.

It might indeed be claimed that there is no such thing as an East Anglian dialect, for there are differences not only between Norfolk and Suffolk but between various parts of the two counties. For the purposes of this book, however, it has been considered appropriate to deal with the region as a whole rather than with just one county.

The maps in *An Atlas of English Dialects*, published in 1996, show clearly the variations that exist within the East Anglian dialect area. Taking account of pronunciation, grammar and words, the maps show that the dialect spoken in Eastern England varies in some respects more from east to west than from north to south; in North and East Norfolk and East Suffolk puppy is the common word for a young dog, for instance, but in South-west Norfolk and West Suffolk pup is more commonly used.

*   *   *

Published glossaries of East Anglian dialect tend to be full of words which are, it has to be said, no more than mispronunciations of common words, or perhaps in some cases variant pronunciations. Major Moor in his glossary includes "shew or shue" for shoe, but this is nothing more than an instance of the East Anglian habit of changing the vowel sound in certain words. I have taken care to exclude, so far as possible, those words which are mere variants in pronunciation of words in common usage.

Care is needed, however, to differentiate between mere differences in pronunciation and older forms of current words. As will be seen, the word "afeard" is not simply a variant pronunciation of "afraid" but is a much older form derived from Anglo-Saxon which might have had a different meaning in Shakespeare's time from the similar word derived from the French.

Afeard is also an example of an archaic word found in country speech all over Britain, but often misidentified as being specifically East Anglian. A study of Joseph Wright's *English Dialect Dictionary* shows how comparatively few terms East Anglia can really claim as her own, for many of those that we accept as being part of our dialect are found also in other regional dialects. Generally words found in Forby, Moor and other lists that prove to be common to many dialects, or in common usage throughout the country, have been omitted from the current book, but in the case of afeard the compiler relented.

Until the Rev Walter Skeat and the English Dialect Society began the work which led to the publication between 1898 and 1905 of *The English Dialect Dictionary* most dialect collectors were working more or less in isolation, so it is not at all surprising that the compilers of East Anglian glossaries were misled sometimes into claiming more than is our due share. Major Moor and John Greaves Nall both point to words shared with Scots and other dialects, but they were probably unaware of just how generally some of the expressions were to be found over a wide area.

The Rev Robert Forby takes up considerable space in explaining the words cant, with various meanings, and cant-rail. A glance at the *Oxford English Dictionary* is sufficient to convince one that these words do not belong to East Anglian dialect but are in common usage, and indeed that comparable words are found so widely in other languages that it is uncertain whether the English word comes from Old French or Low German or, in different senses, from both.

Major Moor includes the word loft, an upper apartment, but then observes that it is not local. Perhaps his comment that a "cock loft" is not a place for poultry but rather a small lumber room was the reason for its inclusion; and there are certainly some of the major's entries that, while not otherwise qualifying for inclusion, have proved so interesting that they have been included in this book.

*   *   *

Many of the words and phrases in this book have been culled from Forby, Moor, Spurdens and other similar sources; in such cases the source is often mentioned during discussion of the particular word or phrase. Others have been gathered by the compiler during the past fifty years, from personal experience and sometimes from personal usage.

Words like bishabarnabee and sowbug, milly-moller and pig-hole I knew and used in my boyhood. My mother regularly complained that my bedroom was a pig-hole, and each spring she fyed out the kitchen, if not the whole house. And when I asked what was for tea I would often be told "bread-and-pullet", though in the event the food was never as basic as that, even in wartime.

As a small boy I did not know that these were local terms, not understood all over Britain. It was only as I grew up that I discovered from schoolmasters and others that the language I spoke was non-standard, and that my pronunciation was not "as it should be".

My horizons broadened with National Service postings to Lancashire and Oxfordshire, and then with appointment to a job in one of the country's foremost fishing ports, which brought me up against a completely new language, that of the herring fishing. My list of East Anglian dialect words was expanding fast.

The words beatster and ransacker were still commonly heard at Lowestoft and Yarmouth in the 1950s, when the herring industry was in its final years. The word beatster, for the woman who mended the damaged drift nets, was understood to have its origin in the operation of beating or repairing the nets, but the word ransacker used for a man who set up the nets after beating provided something of a puzzle. The verb to ransack was well known to me, for my mother would talk of ransacking the cupboard when she was searching for her dressmaking scissors or some other item she had mislaid, but why was it used in this sense? It was my old friend Ted Frost, author of *From Tree to Sea*, that superb book on wooden shipbuilding, who gave me the clue, telling me that in the old days when much of the work was done by beatsters as home work the ransacker's job was to seek out the damage and assess the amount of work to be done—he literally ransacked the nets.

With the demise of the herring fishery at Yarmouth and Lowestoft a way of life died out, and with it an occupational dialect that had existed at least since the Middle Ages. Other industries and trades that have now disappeared also had their specialist vocabularies. Indeed, it might almost be said that the East Anglian dialect itself was the language of the old farming community that depended on the horse for power and for transport and for whom life was dominated by the seasons, by barleysel, haysel, and harvest.

Although crowds are attracted to occasional events at which old farming operations are carried on with horses, these are but artificial re-enactments born out of nostalgia for the old ways that have passed away. Country life is not like that any more, and inevitably a language that has so much affinity with a way of life that has gone will itself fall victim to progress.

Greater mobility in the second half of the twentieth century, the widespread reading of national newspapers, listening to radio and watching television, and the need to travel further to find employment, have all tended to dilute the dialect to a point at which it is difficult to determine exactly where a speaker originates from. Until the beginning of the twentieth century it was possible for those with a well-attuned ear to determine not just from which part of the region a person came but even to pin him down to a particular village; some variation in his speech or his accent would provide the vital clue.

The author recalls telling a Scotsman that he lived in Suffolk, and receiving the answer "from your tongue I'd say you came from further north"—north of the River Waveney, in fact.

One fears that the true East Anglian dialect cannot survive for long now that the old way of life has passed away and education, films, television and other influences erode the old ways of speaking. It would be good to know that in another fifty years or so somebody will write about "The East Anglian Dialect of the twenty-first century," but that is probably wishful thinking.

*   *   *

Many of the illustrations are from photographs taken by the pioneer photographer Peter Henry Emerson, sometimes in collaboration with his friend Tom Goodall. Because of the limitations of cameras in the 1880s these are not always quite as unposed as Emerson would like us to believe, yet they do embody the very character of East Anglia in a bygone age.

Emerson had no romantic notions about the countrymen and countrywomen he photographed. "The more we have studied the peasant's life from our point of view," he wrote, "the more fearful does it appear to us. A terrible struggle for the bare necessities of life, often in uncongenial work, from the cradle to the grave, with no leisure, no light, no comfortable old age to look forward to; only work, hard work, and finally to drop exhausted from the plough into the workhouse."

We should remember his words when we look back at the "good old days" when the true, unadulterated East Anglian dialect was the language of the vast majority of people in our region.

A Suffolk countryman sharpening his bagging-iron at the grindstone, photographed by P.H. Emerson in the 1880s. Behind him is the hog-pole, from which pigs were hung to be dressed and cleaned after having been killed.

An East Anglian Dialect Dictionary

Abroad. In East Anglia this does not necessarily mean overseas, which is the generally accepted modern meaning of this word. In Shakespeare's *Henry IV part 2* one of the characters remarks "I'm glad to see your Lordship abroad," and an East Anglian countryman will still use the word in the same sense, out of doors.

The Maldon sailmaker Fred Taylor once told me how he had a brother, but "he went abroad"; he had moved to Burnham-on-Crouch and set up business there. Seamen use the same word for "at sea".

The Rev Edward Gepp in his *A Contribution to an Essex Dialect Dictionary* (1920) describes field-work as **Broad-work**, that is, work done abroad, away from home.

A.O.D. Claxton in his book *The Suffolk Dialect of the Twentieth Century* tells of an old man on his last legs who said meaningfully "Oi'll sune be a-sleepin' abroad".

Act, act up, to. To play the fool.

Addle. Nothing to do with the curate's egg, this word of Norse origin means to thrive or flourish. A field of corn which is looking well and promising to ripen well is said to addle. Thomas Tusser used the word in his *Hundred Points of Good Husbandry*:

> Where ivy embraceth the tree very sore,
> Kill ivy, else tree will addle no more.

Major Moor, in an imitation of the long vowel used in Suffolk, spells it aadle.

This use of the word seems not to be peculiar to East Anglia, but is found in other dialects. In Essex, Gepp tells us, it is used in a similar sense to that used in Norfolk and Suffolk. He adds the examples "That game 'on't addle" (pay, answer), and "that 'on't addle along o'this."

Afeard. An old form of afraid which has survived in the dialect but is not confined to East Anglia; it would not appear here but for the fact that both Major Moor and the Rev Robert Forby as well as later authors include it in their vocabularies.

It is a good example of an archaic word which has survived in country speech all over Britain, but which is often identified, or rather misidentified, as being specifically an East Anglian word.

"An old and good word for afraid," says Moor. "It is still much used in Suffolk; as it is by Shakespeare, and other older writers." Forby goes further and points out that in Chaucer's time there was a difference between afeard and afraid which has been lost; he quotes from *The Canterbury Tales* "This wif was not aferde ne affraide", and suggests that the difference results from their different derivations.

Afeard is clearly of Saxon origin, from the Anglo-Saxon *ferght*, and means affected by fear, in a fright; afraid is from the French *effrayer*, to startle, and therefore signifies put into a fright by some recent cause, he says.

Aftermath. The feed left on meadows or grasslands after having been mown, says Moor. Joseph Wright in his *English Dialect Dictionary* is more explicit in saying that it is the second crop of grass which grows after the field has been mown. Another word used in Suffolk meaning the same thing is rowens; the major notes that Tusser sometimes spells it roughin, but rhymes it with ploughing, while at other times spelling it rowen:

> Corn carried, let such as be poor go and glean;
> And after thy cattle, to mouth it up clean;
> Then spare it for rowen till Michael be past,
> To lengthen thy dairy no better thou hast.

It might look idyllic in P.H. Emerson's photograph, but this mix of land and water was a good breeding ground for the mosquito that spread ague, or a-gah as it was commonly pronounced.

Agin. The common pronunciation of again or against. The Rev W.T. Spurdens also gives *aginst*, but this is unknown; Major Moor rightly says that Aginn, as he spells it, replaces against "in its several senses". For one sense see the title of Basil Slaughter's little book *Let's Git Up Agin The Table*, a social history of diet and cooking in Essex and East Anglia (1992).

Aggravate. To irritate, as in "Du stop aggravatin' me, child, dun't you'll get a ding o' th' lug!"

A-gah. Major Moor gives this pronunciation for what is in ordinary English called ague, a form of malaria, *Plasmodum vivax*, spread by the mosquito *Anopheles maculpennis* that was once common in marshy areas of East Anglia and Essex, including the Broads and the coastal marshes. Besides causing the deaths of many marsh dwellers this disease was almost certainly responsible for the deaths of James I and Oliver Cromwell. It is probable that the improved drainage of the marshes during the nineteenth and twentieth centuries reduced the mosquito population, though *Anopheles maculpennis* is still present on the Broadland marshes. The reduction of the mosquito population linked with modern preventative medicine to wipe out ague in this country, but it still occurs in northern Holland.

Ah. The Essex form of yes. "The local equivalent of *aye*, which is not used," says the Rev Edward Gepp.

Ail. An awn of barley (Essex); pronounced as in the aisle of a church.

Alegar. A form of vinegar made from beer.

Ale stall. The horse or stool on which casks are placed in the cellar. The word stall is derived from an Old Norse word for a supporting slab or pedestal. The term is commonly found in seventeenth-century inventories.

Alexandra plover. Kentish plover, seen as a passage migrant on the East Coast. It does not now breed either in East Anglia or Kent, in spite of its name.

All mander o' what. All kinds of bits and pieces gathered together, as in many a garden shed; a variation of all manner of things.

All right. The meaning differs with the expression given to the phrase. Said with an expression of doubt, it can mean that something is acceptable but no more; with no particular emphasis, it means satisfactory; with emphasis on the *right* it can mean either that something is first rate or that it is considered something of an imposition. "Thass all *right*, that is, he reckon we ought to work for him and pay him for the priv'lege!"

All up a' Arridge. Just why the port of Harwich should be used in this way to describe a muddle is unknown. A man who was finding nothing going right might say "I fare t' be all up a' Arridge t' mornin'".

Alliwig. The earwig. This word is to be found only in the Rev W.T. Spurdens' supplement to Forby's vocabulary. Major Moor notes the Suffolk name as Arrawiggle, and A.O.D. Claxton lists airy-wiggle for this insect, which appears to be no more than humorous mispronunciation of the kind particularly loved by children. However, it is a mispronunciation that has remained remarkably constant for well over a century. Some East Anglian mispronunciations might have given Edward Lear an idea or two.

Along of. Simply translated as *with*, but this expression is often used in senses that cannot be so simply rendered. "Do you come along o' me" might be said by an old-time policeman apprehending some minor miscreant, or by a youngster who wants to show his friend a new-found nest; in quite a different sense "he ails cruel along o' his head" might be said of a sufferer from migraine.

American weed. Water thyme or Canadian pondweed (*Elodea canadensis*), an alien plant which has become widespread in streams and ditches.

Annind. On end. Not exactly a dialect word, but rather an instance of the East Anglian habit of running two words together and changing the vowel. It could be said of a horse: "'A reared right up annind"—on its hind legs.

Apple Jack. A whole apple, cored but not peeled, baked in a coat of pastry. Moor says it is the same thing as an Apple John, a flapjack or an apple turnover, but perhaps he did not do his own cooking; an apple turnover is made with peeled and cut-up apples, placed on a bed of pastry which is

Army slang, or dialect?

Doubtless the language was to some extent enriched by those who fought the King's wars on the Continent of Europe and in far-off continents such as India. Certainly many words that have been quoted as being part of East Anglian dialect were brought back by men who served the Honourable East India Company, men like Major Edward Moor who when he returned to his native Suffolk after many years in India began to record a dialect that he found both unfamiliar and yet strangely familiar after so long an absence.

While servicemen spoke of an easy job as a "cushy number" East Anglian children used the word "cushies" for sweets; "kushie" is a Hindustani word for something soft and sweet. Another Hindustani word that arrived in East Anglia in the nineteenth century or earlier is "pani", meaning rain. And of course "char" is more than service slang for tea, it has entered the English language.

These words introduced from an Oriental language do not qualify as true dialect words. Indeed, such words are likely to be found in use in any district in the British Isles from which men were recruited for regiments based in India.

then turned over the pieces before being baked. More recently the term apple jack has been used of the toffee-apple, an apple speared on a rough stick and coated with hard toffee.

Apple-pie. Hemp agrimony (*Eupatorium cannabinum*) in Norfolk, but the Rev Edward Gepp found that in his part of Essex, not far from Dunmow, it was the great willowherb (*Epilobium hirsutum*).

Argufy. To argue, or to have some significance, some weight as an argument. Forby gives as an example, "What does that argufy?"

Arps. Tufted ducks.

Arse. The backside, or to a wherryman the tail of a block. Indeed, the bottom part of almost anything; the arse-board, the tail-board of a cart. From an eighteenth-century manual of husbandry one learns that sheaves of corn were laid "in a sloping posture, close together, with their arses out-ward". The *Oxford English Dictionary* says that the word is obsolete in polite speech, but it has certainly survived in the dialect with no trace of self-consciousness. It is a very ancient word with its roots in Old English, Old Norse, Old High German and other teutonic languages, and was not considered at all impolite until the eighteenth century.

Arse-end. The butt of a felled tree.

Arse uppards. As Claxton puts it, "a term used for many things which are placed or lying bottom upwards, or upside down."

Arsle. To move backwards, from *arse*. To arsle is also to fidget; a mother might say to a restless child who will not sit still on his chair, "Oh, do stop arseling about, will ye!"

Arseling pole. Recorded by Forby as a pole with which bakers spread the hot embers to all parts of the oven, otherwise known as a **wrastling pole**.

Arsey-varsey. A "dialect" version of the Latin vice versa. Whether this is genuine dialect is a matter of doubt; it seems far more likely to have been the fabrication of an educated person aiming to produce comic dialect. It is perhaps not without significance that while Claxton includes it among the Suffolk dialect of the twentieth century neither Forby nor Moor recorded it in the nineteenth.

Arternune farmer. A lazy farmer, one who does not get up early enough in the morning to begin work until the afternoon.

Ashel, to. To cut bricks to form a joint in masonry, says William Waters in *Norfolk Archaeology*, 1879. Perhaps this verb is derived from the term *ashlar*, hewn or shaped stone used in building.

Ask. To publish the banns of marriage. Though today we speak of publishing the banns, *ask* is the historical word, used also of proclaiming the loss of cattle. While in 1450 we find "Aske the banns thre halydawes", in the following century we learn that "They ought to ask them thre sondayes in thre or four next parysshe churches and also cry them thre times in thre the nexte market townes"—in the latter case it is stray cattle that are being asked. Gepp records that in Essex when the banns have been read the stipulated three times, the parties are said to have been *out-asked*.

Avel. The awn or beard of barley. The corn was said to be avely if, when dressed for market, the awns adhered to the grains.

Avellong work. Major Moor, as usual, has so apt a definition of this term that one cannot do better than to quote him: Workmen—reapers or mowers—approaching the side of a field not perpendicular or parallel to their line of work, will have an unequal portion to do—the excess or deficiency is called "avellong work". It is a word of Scandinavian origin meaning oblong.

Avise. Simply an obsolete form of advise still much used in East Anglian and, it has to be said, other dialects. Moor gives as an example of its use "Ar yeow awized on't?"

Ax. An old form of the word *ask* still much used by countrymen. Until the sixteenth century *ax* was the regular literary form.

Babbing. A favourite method of fishing for eels on the Broads and elsewhere. A bunch of worms threaded on worsted is fastened to the end of a line, which can be attached to a stick or pole; the line is gently "bobbed" up and down until an eel bites into the bundle of worms. The eel's teeth become tangled in the worsted, and it is possible with care for the eel to be hauled out of the water and shaken into the bottom of the boat or into some receptacle.

William Dutt recalled in *The Norfolk Broads* how a marshman on the Waveney told him "When you feel a little pull at th' line jist hyst it up carefully an' drop th' worams inter th' keeler. Ony you musn't be too hasty about it, or you may shake him orf and luse him. Thas how I mean," he went on as he brought up an eel wriggling on the end of his line, and knocked it off the bab by swinging it against the inside of the tub.

Also known in the west of the region as totting, the outfit of worsted, weight, line and stick being known as a tot.

Bachelor's buttons. The white campion (*Lychnis sylvestris*). "More extensively known by this name than by its trivial appellation, the Campion," says Moor, who refers to bachelor's buttons as "an old name".

Back-striking. A method of ploughing in which the earth turned over by the first ploughing is turned back again. Moor quotes Thomas Tusser:

"Thresh seed, and to fanning," September doth
   cry,
Get plough to the field and be sowing of rye;
To harrow the ridges, ere ever ye strike,
Is one piece of husbandry Suffolk doth like.

By fanning Tusser means winnowing with a fan-shaped flat basket, known as a van.

Back'us. The scullery or wash-house (wash'us) of a farmhouse. The odd-job boy, sometimes an old man rather than a juvenile, was always the back'us boy.

Baffled. In addition to its normal use of hoodwinked or deceived the word is used in East Anglia of standing corn or long grass that has been beaten down by high winds.

Bag. A cow's udder.

Bagging-hook, Bagging-iron. A heavy cutting implement used originally for cutting peas or beans, later for hedge trimming. To bag is to cut corn, peas or beans, as explained in the *Gardener's and Farmer's Vade Mecum* of 1865: "The corn is either reaped, or mown, or bagged. In 'bagging', as it is called, a heavy hook is used: a wisp of straw is cut first and doubled up, or a stick is used instead, held in the left hand, and with the right the heavy hook is driven against the corn close to the ground, and so, by successive strokes, the corn is cut, perhaps a foot deep, up against the standing crop; the wisp or stick in the left hand serving to guide it to a standing place."

"A stiff pull" was the title P.H. Emerson gave to this photograph of a wheel plough, or "star-gazer," at work in a Suffolk field. Such a plough needed a skilled ploughman to set it and use it correctly.

Bail. The bow made of supple wood tied to a scythe handle when mowing barley to hold the corn and deposit it in suitable bundles for gathering as sheaves.

Bait. A meal or snack, or the food taken at a meal. It was used particularly of the mid-morning snack in the fields, and was also used as a verb, to bait the horses, or to give them their oats. In earlier times this word was used of a pause in a journey at an inn both for refreshment and for rest; Samuel Pepys records in his diary on 24th February, 1660, "At Puckeridge we baited, where we had a loin of mutton fried and were very merry". It is another word of Norse origin.

Bait his maggots. A Suffolk way of saying "attend to his fancies". Claxton quotes a Suffolk woman speaking of her husband: "My owd man is hully partikler about what he ate, Oi hev t' bait his maggots."

Balm, to. An Essex word meaning to smear with sticky material or dirt, as in "He's took an' got his fingers balmed all over a sticky." The adjective **balmy** is used of anything so smeared; potatoes that have been dug from wet heavy soil, with earth adhering to them, are so described.

Bandy-wicket. A game played with bat and ball, like cricket. But, says Major Moor, sticks were often used instead of a bat and bricks or, in their absence, hats in place of stumps and bails. Forby also mentions a game called **Bandy-Hoshoe**, played with a *bandy* either made of some very tough wood or shod with metal or with the point of the horn or hoof of some animal.

"The ball is a knob or gnarl from the trunk of a tree, carefully formed into a globular shape," says Forby. "The adverse parties strive to beat it with their *bandies*, through one or other of the goals placed at proper distances. It is probably named from the supposed resemblance of the lower end of the *bandy*, in strength or curvature, to a horse-shoe; or it may be so called from being

shod, as it were, with horn or hoof. In particular, the empty hoof of a sheep or calf, which is frequently used, may be well assimilated to a shoe."

It sounds like a crude form of hockey, and was almost certainly not peculiar to East Anglia.

Bang. A Suffolk cheese made from skimmed milk. It had a particularly bad reputation, and was said by one writer to serve better as ammunition for cannon than for eating; but not all Suffolk cheese was so hard and inedible. Such cheese was also known, in Norfolk at least, as **Thump**, perhaps from the noise it made if dropped on the floor.

Banje, to. To drizzle. An Essex word; the Rev Edward Gepp gives the example, "Tain't rainin'; that's only banjin' a little."

Bar-cutter. A short-handled implement with a blade set in the same plane as the handle, used by marshmen to cut back the *shore* of a dyke.

Bargain. Either the load of a waggon or an indefinite quantity. In his *The History and Antiquities of Hawsted and Hardwick* (1784), one of the earliest parish histories, the Rev Sir John Cullum quotes "I have a good bargain of corn this year", and "a good bargain of lambs". Moor mentions also the other sense in "I'd three bargains off 'a that there small filld", that is, three waggon loads.

Bargoose and bargander. Shelduck, female and male. See also **Bay-duck**.

Barley bird. The nightingale. In Essex, however, the name was used for the siskin, according to Miller Christy. Both migrants arrived around the time barley was sown.

Barmskin. Originally a leather apron such as that worn by a blacksmith, but in later days an oilskin apron worn by herring fishermen to protect their clothes from the fish scales.

Barra-pig. The smallest pig of a litter. Saying that he had no clue to the origin of barra, Moor interestingly comments that "in the ancient language of India, it means a swine, as it does also in some modern dialects".

Barsel. The season of sowing barley.

Batlins. The loppings, or stowins, of trees used for firing, hedging or hurdle making. When tied up into faggots, says Moor, they are called **Bavens**. The Rev Sir John Cullum calls them **Battlings**. Battling is an obsolete word meaning nourishing to cattle, or fattening; it is hard to see a connection with the branches of trees.

Bay-duck. The shelduck, "from its bright colour, like that of a *bay* horse," says Moor.

Bean-weed. Shining pondweed (*Potamogeton lucens*).

Bear's muck. The Fenman's name for the lower band of sticky peat lying between the layer of buttery clay and the underlying hard blue clay.

Beat, to. To repair a drift net used for herring fishing. The word is descended from the Old English *betan*, to make good or repair. Edward FitzGerald in his *Sea Words and Phrases along the Suffolk Coast* spells the word bete, and notes that bet-ups are mended nets; "one constantly reads printed advertisements of so many new nets, and so many bet-ups for sale", he says. It is a word that Chaucer knew. This is a good instance of an old word that survived only in dialect and in a specific usage; it survived also as a forestry term, with the meaning of replanting an area of wood that had been damaged by high wind.

Beatster. A woman or girl who beats or repairs herring nets. They worked in the beating chambers which formed part of the net stores at Yarmouth and Lowestoft and in the coastal villages; those at Kessingland

were wooden sheds quite different from the Lowestoft variety. Many married women worked at home, either in a garden shed or at the back door; the staple for the beating hook would be fitted to the doorpost. The net would be hung from the iron beating hook, or at Kessingland from a wooden peg in the wall, and the beatster would begin by cutting out damaged sections with her beating knife, a small shutknife, before using her beating needle and cotton to repair the net. A single broken mesh was known as a **sprunk**, two broken meshes together was a **crowsfoot**.

Bedsteadle. Used in Essex for what others call simply a bedstead.

A beatster in a Lowestoft beating chamber deftly repairs the sprunks in a drift net.

Beestings or Beastlings. A cow's first milk after calving. The very first milk is very deep in colour and considered unfit for human consumption, but the second and third milkings were normally brought in by the farmer for the use of his own family, who regarded puddings and custards made from it a particular delicacy. Forby comments that "A beastling pudding is thought superior to one made of common milk". Edward Moor refers also to **Beezlins,** the milk of the third or fourth milking after calving. "It is then particularly sweet and thick, and is deemed strengthening by rustics. It is also called Beezlin milk," Moor adds. Derived from the Old English *biesting*. The term is by no means confined to East Anglia but is in widespread dialect use.

Beevers. The farmworker's afternoon snack, more often referred to these days as "fourses" from the time of day. The word is said to come from the Old French *beivre*.

Two tired farmworkers take advantage of their beevers to have a short rest.

Ben-joltram. The ploughboy's usual breakfast, of brown bread soaked in skimmed milk served in a wooden bowl. Forby conjectures that the word might be "meant to express the joltering of the flatulent mixture in the stomach of the young rustic, when he resumes his labour in the field, after swallowing it".

Betsy-and-Jane. A very small piece of cheese on a small slice of bread.

Betty. A person who fusses over details.

Betty about. To fuss around, often without getting very much done. Anyone who has watched a **Hedge-betty** or hedge-sparrow, otherwise a dunnock, feeding on a path will well understand how this little bird got its local name.

Betty cat. A female cat. This word seems to be used mainly in East Suffolk and Northeast Essex. In Norfolk **Moggy**, a variation of the girl's name Maggie, is used in the same sense.

Billywhit, Williewhit. The barn owl.

Billywitch. The cockchafer or maybug, *Melolontha melolontha*, commonly seen in bumbling flight in May and June. Claxton mentions also the names Butterwitch and Cock-horny-bug for the cockchafer; the latter sounds a better description of the male stag beetle with its enormous antler-like jaws. Neither Forby nor Moor mentions this name for the cockchafer, but Forby has "Billy-wix, s. an owl". Both owls and cockchafers come out as the sun goes down, and one wonders if the name has been transferred from one to another.

Bing. Suffolk term for a manger, from Old Norse *bing-r*, heap. In Swedish *binge* is still used in the sense of heap, but in Danish *bing* now means a bin.

Binns. A term for the deck edge of a wherry.

The overhanging binns were protected by the binn iron, an iron strip with a rounded outside face. The bends were the wales or rubbing strakes employed in shipbuilding in the seventeenth and eighteenth centuries, and the wherrymen's term might well have been derived from this.

Bishabarnabee. Dialect name for the ladybird, said to be a corruption of Bishop Bonner's bee. Bishop Bonner, whose home while rector of the parish is still to be seen at Dereham, having survived the fire which destroyed much of the town in 1581, has an unenviable reputation for having been responsible for the burning of several martyrs during the reign of Queen Mary. No doubt the fiery colour of the tiny beetle's wing cases led to its being given this local name. The German name for a ladybird is Marienkafer, presumably in reference to the Virgin; it might be that the new reference to an unsavoury cleric was an attempt to replace a Roman Catholic name with a stoutly Protestant one. Children used to chant the rhyme

> Ladybird, ladybird, fly away home,
> Your house is on fire,
> Your children are gone.

Another name for this insect in Suffolk was golden-bug. Major Moor delightfully quotes a variation of the same rhyme:

> Gowden-bug, Gowden-bug, fly awah home—
> Yar house is bahnt deown an yar children all gone.

In all probability this rhyme had its origin in a more pointed reference to the scandalous behaviour of the Bishop of London in arranging for the burning of his religious opponents.

Blackcap. There is a bird properly known as the blackcap, but in Norfolk the name was also used for the marsh tit.

Black curlew. The glossy ibis, a bird which has been occasionally seen in East Anglia over the years. The Rev Richard Lubbock in his *Observations on the Fauna of Norfolk* (1845) says that "fifty years back it was seen often enough to be known to gunners and fishermen as the Black Curlew".

Black poker. The tufted duck.

Black star. Bog rush (*Schoenus nigricans*).

Black-weed. Bur reed (*Sparganium ramosum*).

Blare. To cry loudly, a word taken directly from the Dutch *blaren*, to cry. Losing patience with a tetchy child, a mother will say "Oh, do stop yer blaren, do!"

Blare and hair. A shipbuilding term for a mixture of coal tar, Stockholm tar, Russian tallow, resin and pitch heated and stirred together, used where two pieces of timber fayed together; cow hair was thrust into the mixture to congeal it and prevent it running away.

Blea. Land flooded just enough for the water to be visible through the grass is said in the Fenland to be blea.

Blind man's holiday. Twilight.

Blood ulph. The bullfinch.

Bloring. The bellowing of a cow. Moor says that "blore is rather applicable to the moaning of a cow after her severed calf—one of the dismallest of rural sounds: or of the wennel [a weaned calf] after her dam." The word appears not to be in common use throughout Suffolk, but is known only in the eastern part of the county.

Blue darr. The black tern, a passage migrant seen in spring and autumn. The second element of the name might be derived from dart.

Blue hawk. The male hen harrier, which is of a distinctive blue-grey colour.

Bluff, to. To cough. At Lowestoft I have heard it said of a person with a bad cold "He's wholly a-blawfin and a-cawfin".

Boar-thistle. The spear thistle (*Carduus lanceolatus*).

Bodikins! An expression of surprise, says Spurdens. Its origin shows that this exclamation is not confined to dialect, or at any rate not to East Anglia, for it is a shortening of **Odsbodikins**. In the Middle Ages there were many common oaths such as "By God's Body!" and "By God's Blood!" After the Reformation, and particularly in the seventeenth century when the Puritans held sway, such profanation of sacred names was frowned on and expressions of this kind were disguised by omitting the initial "G", and sometimes by the addition of some meaningless ending. There is the origin,

These workers coming home from the marshes, seen in a photograph by P.H. Emerson, might well have been cutting bolders with the meaks they carry over their shoulders.

surely, of odsbodikins, which as youngsters we used as a humorous expletive without the slightest knowledge of what the expression really meant. There is also the expression Strewth! which began as God's Truth. And what about **Dogsbody**, or is that something altogether different? There is an expression "to put on dog", meaning to assume pretentious airs. Is a dogsbody not a self-important nobody?

Boke load. Wherryman's term for a cargo which is loaded up above the hatches. A wheelbarrow would sometimes have the sides extended by **boke-boards**, enabling a bigger load to be carried.

Bolder. The true bulrush (*Scirpus lacustris*), formerly cut on the Broads for rush weaving and similar purposes. In 1879 William Waters referred to this as **Bowder rushes**.

Bonka. Fine or strapping when applied to young people, especially to girls, or large when applied to objects such as apples, turnips, etc. Moor knew only of the word being used in the sense of "What a bonka that there mawtha dew grow", and it might be that the second sense, recorded by Claxton, is a twentieth-century extension.

Boodle. The corn marigold (*Chrysanthemum segetum*), a common weed of arable land, and according to Thomas Tusser the worst.

> The May-weed doth burn, and the thistle doth fret;
> The fitches pull downward both rye and the wheat;
> The brake and the cockle, be noisome too much,
> Yet like unto boodle, no weed there is such.

Corn cockle (*Agrostemma githago*), mentioned in this piece by Tusser, has now almost disappeared. See also **Buddle**.

Bootmaker's holiday. Monday. The Rev J.B. Clare in *Wenhaston Records* quotes the following: "Shummakers mak St Monday [regard it as a saint's day and take a holiday]; dew a

"Broad Norfolk"

There being so much nineteenth-century enthusiasm for dialect, it was to be expected that it should erupt into a correspondence in one of the daily newspapers that had begun circulating in the region. A gallimaufry of letter-writers, for the most part using initials or pen-names such as "Octionary", "A Norfolk Woman" and "Pharoah", sent their lists of words, their stories and their observations to the *Eastern Daily Press*, whose editor, Cozens-Hardy, was keen to help preserve "the scores of little 'natives' which in all human probability the Board Schools will have killed in a generation".

The first letter was published in the last issue of 1892, and many more poured in throughout January, 1893. By the end of the year they had all been reprinted in a little book called *Broad Norfolk*, but little effort had been made to sort out the mass of information, and some misinformation, contained in those letters.

More than fifty years later another eruption of letters in the same newspaper demonstrated that neither state education nor changes in rural life had entirely eradicated the Norfolk dialect. It began with a letter containing a list of local names for common wild birds, and quickly grew into an avalanche of correspondence. Later in 1949 Jonathan Mardle (Eric Fowler) contributed an introduction to a booklet entitled *Broad Norfolk, second edition* in which were reprinted, in whole or in part, 270 of the 420 letters received, together with an article on "Craft Vocabularies" by A.J. Forrest.

"This second edition of *Broad Norfolk* is presented to the readers of the *Eastern Daily Press* in the hope that fifty years hence they or their children may write a third one," wrote Jonathan Mardle.

---

little on Tuesda'; wark hud on Wednesda' and Tharsda'; begin to clear up on Frida' an' Sarrada'."

Bor. A common term of address among men. It has been linked with *boy*, but it is much more likely that it is derived from the Dutch *buur* or *buurman*, neighbour.

Bottle-bump. The bittern. The second element of the name is descriptive of the male bird's boom. Sir Thomas Browne wrote of the "Bittor" that "maketh that mugient noyse, or as we term it Bumping by putting its bill into a reed, as most believe". In fact the bittern has no need to use a reed as megaphone; Henry Stevenson writes of a Hoveton man who "surprised a bittern in a reed bush, in the very act of booming, with its head and neck straight up, as one might naturally suppose, and not buried in the mud or the hollow of a reed stem, after the quaint conceit of former naturalists."

Bottle tom. Long-tailed tit, also known as the *Featherpoke* from its meticulously made nest.

Bottom-fying. A term used for cleaning out mud and rotting vegetation from a dyke.

Botty. Proud and snobbish; usually applied to the womenfolk, but can also be used of petty officials who "git above theirselves".

Bout. A turn in ploughing. "Four bouts to the yard" means that the plough turns over nine inches in width in making each furrow.

Bowl. A wooden cask or barrel used as a float for herring and mackerel nets before the introduction of canvas buffs.

Brakes. Bracken (*Pteridium aquilinum*).

Bramble finch. The brambling.

Brattle, to. Forby tells us that this is to lop the branches of a felled tree. **Brattlings** are the loppings from a felled tree.

Brawtches, brotches. Otherwise broaches, those split rods of willow or hazel, sharpened at each end, twisted and bent in the middle and used by thatchers to secure the rods or rizzers that hold down the thatch. In some parts of England known as spars. "A fell of such wood is divided into hurdle-wood and broach-wood," Forby tells us; the former is

the stouter rods, the latter the more slender. In a fifteenth-century source we find "Broche for a thacstere".

Bread-and-cheese. The fruit or seed of the mallows, eaten by children, according to Claxton. Also used in reference to the tender green shoots of the hawthorn, another favourite with children.

Bread-and-pullet. Dry bread with nothing spread on it. A child seeking a piece of bread and jam might be told "The jam's all gone, you'll hatta hev some bread-and-pullet" (bread and pull it).

Bret. A rough apron of hessian or pickling worn by women. Also known as a mantel.

Brew. The edge of a ditch away from the hedge.

It was usual for the buck of an East Anglian postmill to be painted white, as with this example at Leavenheath in Suffolk.

Brewer's apron. Inferior beer, thin as the water the brewer's apron was washed in.

Broad arrow. Arrowhead (*Sagittaria sagittifolia*).

Brow, to. To clear away rough grass and brambles. **Browings** are the results of such work, usually collected and burnt.

Brummagem pilot. A fisherman who acted as a pilot but had no licence from Trinity House authorising him to pilot ships. When no licensed pilot was available a Brummagem pilot might provide a most useful service, even saving a ship whose master was lost among the sands of the East Anglian coast; but the official pilots often complained of the Brummagems taking their bread out of their mouths. The reference to Birmingham is most likely raised by the cheap and ill-made metal goods produced in that burgeoning industrial town in the nineteenth century.

Brush, to. To cut or trim a hedge or bank. **Brushings** are the twigs that result from the operation, as in *brushwood*. A French origin is usually ascribed to the word *brush*, but in this case one might do better to look to the northern European languages.

Buck. The body of a waggon or cart, or the body of a postmill.

Buckheading, buckstalling. A manner of managing hedges in which the growth is cut down to within two or three feet of the ground. William and Hugh Raynbird, who describe this operation in their book *On The Agriculture of Suffolk*, suggest the word might derive from the resemblance of the jagged and forky ends of the stems to antlers; a buckstall was a net used in the sixteenth and seventeenth centuries to catch deer. Nathaniel Kent in his *General View of the Agriculture of the County of Norfolk* (1796) includes buckstalling in his chapter on "Reprehensible Practices"; his opinion was that it caused irreparable damage to the hedge "by checking the growth, and making it hollow at the bottom".

Buddle. The corn marigold (*Chrysanthemum segetum*), a common weed of arable land.

Buff. A large inflated canvas or later plastic float employed with herring drift nets. In earlier days a **bowl**, a small cask or barrel, was used for the same purpose.

Bulk, to. To throb, as in "My poor ol' hid dew hully bulk".

Bull's noon. Midnight. "The inhabitants of dairy counties can feelingly vouch for the propriety of this term," says Forby. "Their repose is often broken in the dead of night by the loud bellowing of the lord of the herd, who, rising vigorous from his evening rumination, rushes forth on his adventures, as if it were broad noon-day, and *blores* with increased rage and disappointment when he comes to a fence which he cannot break through."

Bully. A man standing on the stack who receives the corn pitched up from below. As the stack rose and it became impossible for the pitcher to reach the top of the stack he stood in the bully hole half way up the stack.

Bullymung. A coarse, thick mixture of oats and pease or similar. Thomas Tusser specifically mentioned oats, pease and vetches. To the Rev Sir John Cullum at Hawsted in the eighteenth century it was pease and oats sown together.

Bulrush. Local name for the greater reedmace (*Typha latifolia*). The true bulrush (*Scirpus lacustris*) or club-rush is known in Norfolk as **bolder**.

Bumbazzle. A beating; it sounds like the word bamboozle, and might be related, though the meaning is rather different.

Bumby. The little shed at the bottom of the garden, otherwise known as the privy. Forby records that the word was also used of any collection of stagnant filth, while the Rev Sir John Cullum defines it as "a quagmire, from stagnating water, dung, etc., such as is often seen in farm-yards". The Rev Edward Gepp defines it as being in Essex a refuse pit; all shades of the same meaning.

Bunds. Knapweed (*Centaurea nemoralis*).

Bunk. Marsh angelica (*Angelica sylvestris*).

Bunny. A swelling from a blow, "especially from a schoolmaster's ruler," adds Major Moor somewhat ruefully. John Steele's manuscript (about 1712) in the Bodleian Library contains another word, **Bown**, for a swelling or bump; "is this connected with bun, a cake of a swelling shape?" asked the Rev Greville J. Chester, who published a list of "Norfolk Words not in Forby's Vocabulary" in the original papers of the Norfolk and Norwich Archaeological Society in 1857. That is questionable, but certainly it seems possible that the word *bown* could over the course of time be corrupted into *bunny*.

Bush. A thorn; in Suffolk a man would speak of having a bush in his finger, which could sometimes be very painful.

Bush faggot. A faggot of hawthorn or blackthorn.

Bush-weed. The water crowfoots (*Ranunculus* spp).

Buskins. A covering for the legs worn by farmworkers employed in muddy fields or in the mire of the farmyard. Buskins could be made of any kind of waterproof material, and fastened in several places down the side. Makeshift buskins could take the form of sacking wrapped around the legs and fastened with binder twine. The shaped leather leg coverings worn by superior workers such as farm stewards, gamekeepers and chauffeurs were known as "leggings".

Busky-oo. The call which brought fishermen up from below to haul the nets.

Butcher-bird. The red-backed shrike (*Lanius collurio*), so called from its habit of impaling its prey on thorns. This name is almost certainly not local to East Anglia, and W.B. Lockwood in *The Oxford Dictionary of British Bird Names* shows that it is not a genuine folk name but rather a name adopted by early naturalists.

Buttle. A bittern. Also sometimes called a **bottle-bump**, q.v.

Buttonhole flower. *Montia perfoliata*, an alien weed which has spread rapidly in this century and is particularly abundant in the Breckland. The name almost certainly arises from the small white flowers springing from the centre of the leaf, as though in a buttonhole.

Buzzhawk. The nightjar, otherwise known to many Suffolk people as the sewing-machine bird, from its peculiar song at dusk. See also **Dorhawk**, **Goatsucker**.

Cackle, queckle. Suffocate. Ashley Cooper in *Heart of Our History* (1994) quotes Jack Cornell, of Bulmer, near Sudbury, talking of the local pub, the Cock and Blackbirds: "Makes you laugh to think of it though, but on a Sunday night in the tap room, Uncle Harry Rowe would cut some bacca up with a shut knife and there would be him and two or three old men with these 'ere clay pipes on the go! Well, talk about the smoke! It was enough to cackle you!" Going back into the eighteenth century, there was an occasion when a cache of smuggled goods was buried on the Essex coast in the vicinity of Great Holland; unhappily when the time came to remove the goods the air in the vault had become foul, and two men who went down into it were "queckled".

Cad. In Essex the smallest pig in a litter, perhaps an abbreviation of *cadet*, a younger son.

Callerbot. An Essex name for a young rook.

Camping pightle. The Rev Sir John Cullum of Hawsted mentions in his history a deed of about 1500 referring to "The camping pightel joined to the East side of the churchyard" that was let for 13s.4d. a year. It was a small close used for playing the game rather than for living under canvas. Today there is still a piece of land in Stowmarket known as The Camping Land. See David Dymond: "A Lost Social Institution: The Camping Close" in *Rural History* 1 (1990) pp. 165–192.

Cankers. The fruit of the wild rose, otherwise known as hips. Originally the word was used for the dog-rose: in Shakespeare's *Henry IV Part 1* we have "To put downe Richard, that sweet lovely rose, and plant this thorne, this Canker Bullingbrooke".

Canker rose. The Corn poppy (*Papaver rhoeas*), before the days of spraying an abundant weed in cornfields, sometimes known as red-weed.

Cankerweed. Common ragwort (*Senecio jacobaea*), a plant that can prove very poisonous to cattle and other animals when growing in pastures. According to Forby it was in the eighteenth century so abundant in Suffolk that it was collected from the commons and waste lands and burned for the making of potash.

Caper-plant. Caper spurge (*Euphorbia lathyris*), a common weed of gardens. Forby explains that it was so called from a fancied resemblance of its capsules to capers. "The substitution is known to have been once at least tried by a remarkably frugal housewife," he says. "Fortunately, the first acrimonious taste warned the family to reject the noxious sauce, and they escaped with a little excoriation of lips and tongue."

Capple. The wooden loop on a flail by which the swingel is attached to the handstaff.

Carnser, carnsey. A causeway across low-lying or marshy land, or a raised pathway. Forby spells it Caunsey, which brings the word a step nearer to its apparent Latin derivation.

Carr. Wet, marshy woodland containing mainly alder. Natural succession is for open water to silt up until a depth is reached at which reed and rush can grow; reedbeds form and then unless the reeds are managed alders and birches will seed, in time forming carr.

Cast, to. To yield, to produce. Forby gives as an example "How did your wheat cast?", and then adds that in Suffolk the question would be "How did it rise?"

Cat's-tail, Foxtail. The Mare's-tail (*Hippuris vulgaris*), a plant found growing in wetland and in water, said to be a descendant of a plant family that was prolific in prehistoric times, perhaps when the dinosaurs roamed the earth. Linnaeus gave it the name *Hippuris*, from hippo, the Latin for horse, but Forby remarks "here we must correct the great naturalist; this plant is surely more like the tail of a cat than that of a horse".

Cauliflower weed. Water crowfoot (*Ranunculus* spp).

Caunsey. See **Carnser**.

Cavings, calder. The refuse of threshed corn, broken ears, chaff and dust ejected at the side of the threshing drum; or in earlier days, the refuse left in the caving-sieve after dressing corn.

The fatal sport of Camping

Camping was a game which, in spite of the periodic banning of such sports, was popular in East Anglia. Various descriptions of this notoriously rough game have been given, including one by P.H. Emerson, the pioneer photographer, in his *Pictures of East Anglian Life*, published in 1888.

"This is a kind of mixed hockey and football, the ball used, however, being seven inches in diameter, and soft. Each player had a stick to strike the ball with, and at each end of the field were placed the byes or goals, made by placing bent osier twigs into the ground so as to form arches. Both sides—the number on each side being unlimited, ten a side, however, being a common team—had to toe the goal-line. One 'starter' then took the ball and placed it in the middle of the field, covering it with his hat. The removal of this hat was the signal to begin, and forthwith the fleetest runners rushed to the ball to get the first stroke, whilst the field took up their allotted positions. The players were allowed to throw and run with the ball, but not to kick it. The game, we are told, was very rough, and sparring men and bullies were often hired on both sides. These matches, organised as a rule by the publicans, frequently took place between neighbouring villages and hundreds, the field often being lined with waggons."

The Rev. W.T. Spurdens remarks that "The camping of which Mr. Forby writes is beginning to be forgotten, and it is well. The contests were, not unfrequently, fatal to many of the combatants. I have heard old persons speak of a celebrated camping, Norfolk against Suffolk, on Diss Common, with 300 on each side. Before the ball was thrown up, the Norfolk side enquired tauntingly of the Suffolk men, if they had brought their coffins! The Suffolk men, after 14 hours, were the victors. Nine deaths were the result of the contest, within a fortnight!"

Chance child. An Essex term for an illegitimate child.

Char-hole. The place in the roof of a stack in which a man stands to take the corn from the man below him. Neither Forby nor Moor gives this word, but it is included by William Waters in a list in *Norfolk Archaeology* Vol VIII (1879).

Chatter-pie. A magpie, a clear allusion to its harsh chattering call.

Cheat. The sedges (*Carex riparia* and *C. acutiformis*), reed canary-grass (*Phalaris arundinacea*) and other grasses and sedges regarded as "small stuff" present on a marsh cut primarily for reed.

Chig, chig. A call of invitation to pigs, says the Rev. Greville J. Chester in *Norfolk Archaeology*, Vol V.

Chimbley. A variant pronunciation of chimney, one of several to be found in dialect use. *An Atlas of English Dialects* (1996) charts four variations, chimbley, chimley, chimbey and chimdey, used in East Anglia; experience suggests that chimbley is by no means confined to the area of West-central Norfolk to which it is reserved on map 73.

Church-hole. One's last resting place, the grave.

Clocks. A name used by fishermen in North Norfolk for dead mussels, often those that have been opened by oystercatchers. When shaken the shells make a sound like an old-fashioned cheap alarm clock.

Clung. Limp, like a cabbage that has been picked and left lying all day in the sun.

Cobble. The stone of fruit such as plums and peaches; also a rounded flint such as one finds on the beaches or in the paving of old streets, but in this sense by no means confined to East Anglia.

Cobs. Gulls. The black-headed gull was sometimes known as a Scoulton cob, from

Cobbles picked off the beach were used for the walls of cottages and other buildings in the coastal areas of Suffolk and Norfolk. These cottages were on the Beach at Lowestoft.

the large colony at Scoulton which was first recorded in the seventeenth century.

Coburg. A wooden wedge-shaped fairing which prevented the mainsheet from fouling the protruding part of the cabin stovepipe on a wherry. The wooden chimney, which might be either a short one or a long one, was made to fit on top of the coburg. It seems likely that the term came into use shortly after the marriage in 1840 of Queen Victoria and Prince Albert of Saxe-Coburg, who also gave his name to a type of bread loaf, a dress fabric and a hat.

Cockey. A drain or sewer. In Norwich the Cockey was a stream running down to the Wensum from the vicinity of the castle; it gave its name to Cockey Lane, now London Street.

Cock-horny-bug. The cockchafer, an insect which has a variety of dialect names. See **Billywitch**.

Cock-up bridge. A descriptive Fenland name for a small lift bridge of the Dutch pattern, with counterbalanced beams which raise the roadway section by means of hanging chains to enable boats to pass through.

Codswallop. Light-hearted nonsense, so called from the fizzy carbonated drink normally purveyed in Codd bottles, those glass bottles sealed with a marble and patented in 1872 by Hiram Codd, a Camberwell soda water manufacturer, and so neither true dialect nor specifically East Anglian.

Crinkle-crankle walls are a feature of Suffolk that present-day bricklayers generally cannot produce. Some modern so-called crinkle-crankle walls have angles instead of curves.

Cop, to. To throw. "Cop me the ball!" might be said by one boy to another. A.O.D. Claxton makes the point that it means specifically to throw underhand or to toss.

Cope, to. To exchange, says J. Steele about 1712. The origin is clearly to be found in Dutch, in which *kopen* is to buy. A *coper* was a nineteenth-century Dutch seagoing gin shop, where North Sea fishermen could obtain drinks and tobacco, sometimes allegedly in exchange for ship's stores belonging to the owner.

Cornelian. Mezereon (*Daphne mezereum*), a rare native plant of wet woodland. See also **Garland flower**.

Cowbird. The yellow wagtail, which was often found among cattle on the marshes feeding on insects attracted by the animals.

The game of Conkers

The Rev Edward Gepp includes the word conker, a horse chestnut, in his list of Essex words, although it is surely in more than local use. On investigation, I discovered that the word *conker* was a dialect word for a snail (it appears in several lists of East Anglian words, though the usual word used for a snail here is hodmedod); and that the game of conkers was originally played by pressing two snail shells together until one of them broke. As it seems to have been played with live snails it is probably just as well that conkers came in the nineteenth century to be played with horse chestnuts, and the word transferred itself to the fruit of the horse chestnut.

Cow mumble. The hogweed (*Heracleum sphondylium*). Together with sheep's parsley (*Anthriscus sylvestris*), hogweed growing in the hedge was gathered as food for rabbits, but children setting out to gather such food were warned of the need to avoid hemlock (*Conium maculatum*), another umbellifer growing along the roadside, which is highly poisonous both to animals and to humans. Because hogweed and sheep's (or cow) parsley were gathered together in this way the name cow mumble is often used also for sheep's parsley.

Cow with an iron tail. The pump. A farmer who had a habit of watering down his milk was sometimes said to have such a beast in his herd.

Crab grass. William Waters includes this in a list of "Norfolk Words not found in Forby's Vocabulary" in *Norfolk Archaeology* Vol VIII, explaining it as common sandwort. It is uncertain which of the sandworts this is.

Cradge or scradge bank. The lower bank of a washland river, designed to be overflowed when water levels endanger the outer barrier bank. Rather like an electrical fuse, says Phil Gray, of Whittlesey, it is deliberately included as the weakest link in the system that will give way and prevent greater damage elsewhere.

Cradle. A contraption fitted to a scythe when mowing wheat to hold the corn and deposit it in suitable masses for gathering up as sheaves.

Crane-cutter. An implement with a long blade, slightly curved, set in the same plane as the handle, used to cut down reeds and grasses growing out of water in a dyke.

Cratch. A rack holding fodder for horses or cattle. From the Middle English *crecche*, a manger or crib.

Creeping Sarah. A descriptive name for Wall-pepper (*Sedum acre*), one of the stonecrops, which creeps its way over banks and walls and across heathland.

Cringled, crinkled. Irregular, shrunk, shrivelled or crumpled, like Major Moor's favourite carrots (See under **Lunnunners**).

Crinkle-crankle wall. A form of garden wall found mainly in Suffolk. Only one brick thick, and with no buttresses although at least six feet in height, the wall gained its strength from its serpentine shape. Fruit trees were sometimes planted within the curves of the wall to gain the advantage of the shelter provided. A particularly impressive crinkle-crankle wall, described by Norman Scarfe as "the longest ribbon wall in the world", can be seen at Easton, near

Wickham Market, though this has been breached to provide access to modern housing built in what had been the grounds of the home of the Dukes of Hamilton.

Crome. A long-handled implement with tines set at right-angles to the shaft, used for hauling weed from a dyke or river, and also used for dragging burning thatch from the roof of a house on fire. The word has a Celtic root; crom is the Welsh for crooked, and the right-angled tines might be likened to a crooked fork. A **muck crome** is a similar tool used for raking muck from carts when spreading manure on the fields. See also **dydle**.

Crome stick. A stick cut from the hedgerow with two or three inches of a side branch left at one end as a hook, used when gathering blackberries.

Crow. This name was used indiscriminately for the carrion crow and for the rook. Young boys used to be employed in "crow-scaring", but in fact the birds they were frightening off the crops were rooks.

Crowd. A verb meaning to push a barrow, from the Dutch *kruien* with the same meaning. The term was certainly current in East Anglia in the fifteenth century: Margaret Paston "sent word . . . that sche sculd come hedyr . . . thoow sche sculd be crod in a barwe." Hence a **crudburra** (crowdbarrow) is a wheelbarrow.

Cuckoo barley. Barley which has been planted too late to produce a good crop, i.e. after the arrival of the cuckoo.

Cuckoo flower. The early purple orchid (*Orchis mascula*).

Cuckoo's mate. The wryneck.

Cyprus cat. A tabby cat, but also used in Suffolk of a ginger and white cat. It has been said that reddish-brown cats were called Cyprus cats from having been brought home by the Crusaders from the Mediterranean island.

Dag. Dew. One of those words that has come to us from Scandinavia; in Swedish it is *Dagg*, in Norwegian *Dogg* and in Danish *Dug*.

Dardledumdue. An expressive Suffolk word for someone who is too lazy to do a proper day's work.

Deal apple. A pine cone.

Dean. A morsel. A.O.D. Claxton quotes "There won't a dean in owd Mother Hubbard's cupboard". It is also used in an instruction to a sleepless child: "Don't you make a dean", meaning the slightest sound.

Delf ditch. A ditch alongside a river to carry drainage water into a lower section of the river, below either a mill or a lock. At Flatford there is a dry dock used for repairing Stour barges which drains through a pipe passing beneath the river into the delf ditch on the far side. The word appears to be Dutch *delft*, a ditch.

Develin. The swift. This rather mysterious bird makes itself known to Man as dusk begins to fall, flying at great speed around the rooftops and between the chimneys with shrill screams, while for most of the day and the rest of the night it rests on the wing at a great height; to the superstitious it must indeed have seemed a little devil that appeared from nowhere as night drew nigh.

Dew-drink. The first allowance of beer made to harvesters, taken before they begin the day's work.

Dibbles, debbles. Tools used, one in each hand, for making holes for the setting of corn, beans and peas. See under **Droppen**.

Dicky. Usually pronounced dicka, this is a dialect word for a donkey. Although it is

The Rev Sir John Cullum

For some early researchers the compilation of glossaries went along with an interest in local history. Probably the first to publish his findings was the Rev Sir John Cullum, the squire-parson of Hawsted in West Suffolk, who included a list of words in use in the parish in his *The History and Antiquities of Hawsted in the county of Suffolk*, the first edition of which was published in 1784.

Not only did Sir John Cullum print a list of words, but in the body of his history he recorded other local expressions and local customs, thus providing material for the current dictionary. Sir John, whose book was one of the earliest parish histories to be produced, was buried outside the north door of his church in an effort to persuade his parishioners to follow his example and allow themselves to be buried on the unpopular shady side of the churchyard.

included in the *Oxford English Dictionary*, that authority gives East Anglia the priority, remarking that the word was first noted in East Anglia and Essex; *The Gentlemen's Magazine* in 1783 referred to it as a dialect word used in Essex and Suffolk, providing the dictionary with its earliest example, others coming from Forby, Robert Bloomfield, the Suffolk poet, and Edward FitzGerald.

The well-known Barking Dicky in Westlegate, Norwich, was once a public house known as the Light Dragoon; the ill-painted sign showed a soldier mounted on a horse which appeared to have its mouth wide open, hence the allusion to a barking donkey.

A Norfolk man meeting another in a foreign place might ask "Ha' yar fa'er got a dicka, bor?" to which the correct answer is "Yis, an' he want a fule ter roide him. Will ya come?"

The crudbarras used to load and unload wherries, seen in this photograph of Langley Staithe, near Loddon in Norfolk, were of a peculiar kind. Built without legs, they could be laid down on a plank across the hold for loading.

Dickey-bird. The oyster catcher or sea pie. A dickey was a starched shirt front, and the white chest of the oyster catcher can certainly be likened to a gentleman in a dress shirt.

Didapper. The little grebe, or to give it its alternative common name, the dabchick. No doubt both didapper and dabchick originated in the bird's diving habit; cf dipper.

Dilberries. Pellets of hardened dung hanging in the breech of a sheep.

Dills. The teats of a sow. Typically, Moor tells us that "A pig for every dill" is a good character for a store or breeding sow, while "More pigs than dills" was said of a large family and small means.

Dilver, to. To weary with labour or hard exercise, a word recorded by the Rev Sir John Cullum in the eighteenth century. "I'm quite dilver'd," says a nurse, worn out with watching over a sick person.

Dindle. The dandelion (*Taraxacum officinale*).

Ding. A sharp blow. A ding o' the lug is a box of the ears.

Dinge, dinje. As a noun, light rain; or as a verb, to drizzle. It seems to be a word of Norse origin. Dinjin is the adjective, implying—as Moor tells us—weather unsuitable for hoeing wheat in, as the weeds would not die.

Directly. Immediately, or at least as soon as possible, as in "Thass all right, I'll do that directla."

Do. A whole book might be written on the uses of the word do, sometimes written *du* or even *dew*. Perhaps the best example of the use of the word is a Norfolk labourer's explanation of how his guv'nor rebuked him for some misdemeanour or other: "My master he say, he do, that if I did do as I oughter do I shon't do as I do do, he do." Another good example is: "She dun't do as she oughter do, do she wun't do as she do do." It can be compared to the modern German *doch*, meaning yet, well, or but, and the Danish *dog*, meaning though, yet or even if. For Lord Nelson's use of the imperative do, see the introduction.

Do. As a noun, this means a way of dealing with or treating someone. "A rum ol' do" is a commonly used expression for strange or unfair treatment of someone. The Rev Edward Gepp tells a delightful story of an old man who had imbibed too freely and got his hand stuck in the spout of a pump; addressing the pump, he said "Now then, fair does, owd mate, no howd'n."

Do, to. The phrase "To do for" means to take care of or to provide for someone, as a housekeeper or as a foster parent or in some similar capacity. In quite a different sense, a drunken man might say to someone who has upset him "I'll do for you!" meaning hit him on the head under cover of darkness or dispatch him in some even nastier way.

Dockey. The farmworker's mid-morning bait or snack. He took with him his dockey-bag, which might also be employed to save a choice morsel or two from the horkey after harvest. Today people refer to their doggy bag, making at least the pretence that the morsel being saved is for the dog, not for themselves or their family.

Dodder-grass. Quaking grass (*Briza media*).

Dodman. A snail. The name is said to be derived from the prehistoric surveyor or dodman with his two measuring poles, as seen in various chalk figures; the snail's eye-stalks equate to the measuring poles. See also **Hodmedod**.

Dogweed. Wild cornel; cf dogwood.

Dolver. A Fenland smallholding.

Doolally. "Not quite right in the head", insane. Not truly a dialect word but an example of Army slang that entered the dialect at the time the 9th Foot, the Norfolk Regiment, and the 12th Foot, the Suffolk Regiment, served in India. There was a military lunatic asylum at a place called Devlali or Deolali, and according to the *Oxford Dictionary of Modern Slang* the full form is doolally tap, the word *tap* being Persian for fever.

An interesting Suffolk connection is the local nickname for Walton Battery, a Napoleonic era fortification on the north shore of Harwich Harbour now buried under one of the Port of Felixstowe container terminals. The local name Dooley Fort presumably originated at the period when a posting to such an outpost was liable, in Tommy Atkins' imagination, to send one doolally. The name has since become attached to the public house formerly known as the Walton Ferry Inn.

One who is mad is also said to be **round the bend**. In the nineteenth century when the British Army was on garrison duty in Australia a soldier went berserk and shot the sergeant. It was reported in a Suffolk newspaper that the deranged man had been sent to the military lunatic asylum "at the Yarra Bend", i.e. at a bend in the River Yarra.

Dorhawk. The nightjar. See also **Buzzhawk**, **Goatsucker**.

Dow. The wood pigeon. The word is pronounced to rhyme with cow. It appears to be of Norse origin; the Norwegian for a pigeon is *due*, pronounced *doer*. It could also be a variant pronunciation of dove.

Drain. The Fenland word for a ditch. See also **dyke**.

Drawing match. A ploughing match in which each competitor endeavours to draw a straighter furrow than his rivals, still continuing in the days of tractor ploughing. That pioneer parish historian the Rev Sir John Cullum transcribed an advertisement from the *Suffolk Mercury* of 22nd June, 1724, which reveals that the earlier drawing matches did not involve ploughs.

On Thursday July 29 1724, there will be a Drawing at Ixworth Pickarel, for a piece of plate of 45 shillings value, and they that will bring five horses or mares may put in for it, and they that can draw 20 the best and fairest pulls with their reins up, and then they that can carry the greatest weight over the block with fewest lifts and fewest pulls, shall have the said plate, by such judges as the masters of the teams shall choose. You are to meet at 12 o'clock and put in your names (or else to be debarred from drawing for it) and subscribe half a crown a piece to be paid to the second best team.

Sir John added further explanation, which is certainly required by today's readers. "The trial is made with a waggon loaded with sand, the wheels a little sunk into the ground, with blocks of wood laid before them to increase the difficulty. The first efforts are made with the reins fastened as usual to the collar; but the animals cannot when so confined, put out their full strength: the reins are therefore afterwards thrown loose on their necks, when they can exert their utmost powers, which they usually do by falling on their knees and drawing in that attitude. That they may not break their knees by this operation, the area on which they draw is strown with soft sand."

The Pickerel Inn, now so spelt, still stands in the main street of Ixworth.

Draw-latch. A most expressive compound word for a sneaking fellow who might also be termed an eaves-dropper.

Draw-water. The goldfinch, also known as a *King Harry*. This little bird with its startling colouring was often kept as a cage bird, and in captivity it could be taught to draw water for itself with a thimble and chain, hence the name draw-water.

Dredge. A mixture of oats and barley sown together. Thomas Tusser implies that dredge was commonly grown in East Anglia when he wrote:

> Sow barley and dredge with a plentiful hand.
> Thy dredge and thy barley so thresh out to malt.

Drift, driftway. A road leading from the higher ground on to the marshes along which cattle were driven to the grazing marshes. See also **Drove**.

Driv. Drove, the past participle of *to drive*. "Yow driv yar pigs finely i' the night" was said to a man who snored.

Droppen. This is of course no more than a mispronunciation of the word dropping, but the description given by Major Moor under this heading is so interesting as to be worth reprinting. It is, he says, the operation of dropping grains of wheat, pease or beans into holes made by the dabs or dibbles, wooden implements shod with iron for making the holes in which the seed was set; later dibbles were wholly of iron. Two dibbles were used by a dibbler, one in each hand; the dibbler walked backwards while dabbing. Droppers were always women and children; and as the dibbler generally took the job by the acre, the earnings of a family at this work could be considerable. "It is surprising with what quickness and accuracy dropping is executed by a good dropper," Moor observed. "One will sometimes carry three holes at once; children seldom more than one hole; such portion of work is called a rocket." Before the end of the nineteenth century dibbling and dropping had been rendered obsolete by the seed drill developed by James Smyth at Peasenhall; Major Moor's remarks as to the earnings of a family help to explain the opposition put up by the agricultural workers to the drill operators.

Drove. A Fenland road or track leading to the grazing marshes, much the same as a drift in East Norfolk and North-east Suffolk.

Drug. A four-wheeled vehicle for the conveyance of heavy timber, having the rear axle fitted in such a way that its position can be changed to suit the load being carried. The timber had to be hauled up inclined planks to lay it on the drug; this could be done by parbuckling the log with a horse to haul on the end of the rope. See also **Jim**.

Ducks an' drakes. A game played by children, as Moor explains, "played by casting stones on to the surface of a still piece of water, slantingly, that they may dip and emerge several times." It is perhaps a mark of the old major's character that he had so sharp a memory of his boyhood pastimes. "If once, it is a duck—if twice a duck an' a drake—if thrice, a duck an' a drake an' a fie'penny cake—four times, is a duck an' a drake an' a fie'penny cake an' a penny to pah the baker. If more than four, a duck—a duck an' a drake, &c. are added. These distinctions are iterated quickly to correspond in time, as nearly as may be, with the dips of the stone."

He adds that it might be said of a spendthrift "Ah! he 'av made fine ducks and drakes of a's money—that 'a have."

Dudder, to. To shudder or shiver with either cold or fear.

Duffus. A dovecote. No more than a rendering of the word dove-house, in the same way that backhouse became back'us.

Duller. A noisy child would be told "hold your duller, do". If the child did not quieten down it might get "a ding o' the lug", which might well result in it "blaring".

Dusty-powl. Moor tells of hearing a miller called dusty-powl, explaining that powl is a Suffolk word for the head; it is, of course, a local pronunciation of the word poll, a very old word for the head—hence the poll tax, a per capita levy.

Dutfin, dutphin. A cart horse's bridle.

East Anglia's many dialects

To speak of the East Anglian dialect is misleading, for there is no one dialect spoken throughout the region. Rather are there many variations, not always conveniently aligned with the county boundary, for along the Waveney valley the people speak a dialect that is neither Norfolk nor Suffolk, but a variant that is distinctive enough to mark a speaker as coming from that particular area.

The language spoken in the Broads region of East Norfolk is very different from that spoken around King's Lynn, which has an affinity with the Lincolnshire dialect. And in Suffolk there is a definite difference between the dialects of the eastern and western parts of the county.

It has been said that Suffolk dialect is Norfolk set to music, but this is certainly an over-simplification. It is in the southern part of the county that speakers "sing", their voice rising and falling, the sentence ending on a rising note. The same sing-song way of speaking is to be found along the River Colne in Essex, proving that the Stour estuary is not as much of a natural boundary as is often supposed; it is perhaps significant that the farmers of the Tendring Hundred tend to visit the Suffolk Show, besides having their own local agricultural event, the Tendring Show.

Words and expressions that are familiar in one area are quite unknown in another. Yet there is sufficient uniformity throughout the counties of Norfolk and Suffolk, perhaps, to permit one to speak of the East Anglian dialect.

Duzzy. Stupid, as in "you duzzy owd fule, you!" Spurdens quotes a duzzy-pate. From the Old English *dysigan*, to be foolish; dizzy at first meant just that, and only later came to be applied to a feeling of spinning in the head. The East Anglian word retains the original meaning but the vowel has changed, in normal East Anglian fashion.

Dwile. A floorcloth, a word which has entered the dialect direct from the Dutch, in which it is spelt *dweyl*. The "traditional" sport of dwile flonking, in which a floorcloth is soaked in beer held in a chamber pot and then hurled at the opposing team, is a spoof game introduced in the 1960s and first played in the Bungay area.

Dydle. A long-handled tool with a metal ring at one end on which is fastened a piece of net, used to dredge out mud from a broad or a dyke. The same word is also used as a verb to describe the operation of removing mud using such an implement. It was known to Thomas Tusser, who was born at Rivenhall in Essex about 1524 and farmed at Brantham, overlooking the River Stour:

> A sickle to cut with, a didall and crome
> For draining of ditches that noyes thee at home.

Dyke, dike. A word of Old English origin, also found in Dutch and some other languages, which has come to have two quite dissimilar meanings. In the Broads area of Norfolk and Suffolk, where it is pronounced *deek*, it is normally used of a drainage ditch, but in the Fens and elsewhere it means an earthen bank, as it does in the Netherlands. The Devil's Dyke is an impressive earthwork of indeterminate date stretching from near Newmarket to the fen edge at Reach in Cambridgeshire, and there are other linear earthworks similarly called dykes. In the sense of an earthen bank the word is by no means peculiar to East Anglia.

*Eel-picking on a Suffolk river seen in a photograph by
P.H. Emerson, who records that this was a winter
occupation of the Southwold fishermen.*

Eel pick. A spear which would be driven into
the mud; eels would become jammed between the springy tines. In Norfolk and
Suffolk the pick was made of sheet iron, but
in Essex the tines were of round iron, with
hooked ends. Also known in some areas as
an eel pritch, and in the Fens as a gleave.

Eel sett. A large net spanning a river for the
catching of migrating eels. The net extends
from bank to bank and thus traps all the eels
as they swim downriver on their way to the
sea. The upper part of the net is fastened to
a rope bearing a number of wooden floats
and made fast to a stout pole on each side of
the river, while the foot of the net is fastened
to a second rope, the warp, which is
weighted to hold it firmly to the river

bottom. From the mouth the net tapers into
two, three or four bosoms, to each of which
is attached a pod, a long cylinder of net
stretched tightly over hoops. A line from the
end of each pod enables the fisherman to lift
the pod to remove the catch. It is possible to
lower the net to the river bed to allow vessels
to pass over it. Years ago there were numerous setts on the Broadland rivers, but only
one now survives.

Election. Nothing to do with politics; the Rev
Sir John Cullum records the word in the
eighteenth century in the sense of *likely*, and
as an example gives "We are in election to
have a bad harvest this year".

Elm broth. A Suffolk term for a clout with a
stick.

Esh. An ash tree. The changing of vowels is
common enough in East Anglian speech,
but in this case Forby points out that the
word is derived directly from the Saxon *æsc.*

Every-each. Every other, alternate. Both Forby and Moor include this, the major adding as an example "He preach a sermon every-each Sunday".

Ewe. The past tense of To owe. A countryman, speaking of a debtor, might say "He ewe me ten pound."

Fan. A large basket used in winnowing corn. See also **Van**.

Fare. A much-used dialect word which derives from the same root as the German *fahren*, to go. Forby records it as merely *to seem*, but it is used in a number of other senses which are best detailed by example. A countryman might say of a sickly neighbour "she fare wholly bad" while a comment on the weather might be "thet fare t' be rainin' like thass never goin' t' stop". And as two men part after a night in the local one will say to the other, "Fareyewell, moind how ye goo".

The word was also used in the sense of a journey or voyage. Old documents speak of the mackerelfare, herringfare and sparlingfare, the mackerel, herring and sprat voyages; in this sense the word denotes not just a single trip but the whole season, later generations of fishermen speaking of the herring voyage in the same way.

In Suffolk the phrase "She fare as if!" was often used of a woman who put on airs and graces.

Fen nightingale. A frog.

Fennel-weed. Fennel-leaved pondweed (*Potamogeton pectinatus*).

Ferret's-tail. Hornwort (*Ceratophyllum* spp).

Few. See **Good few**.

Fiddlesticks. Marsh figwort (*Scrophularia aquatica*).

Firetail. The redstart, a bird which is particularly numerous in the Breckland in summer.

Fishleaf. Water plantain (*Alisma plantago-aquatica*).

Fog. The grass ordinarily known as Yorkshire fog (*Holcus lanatus*).

Foisty. Not actually mouldy, but smelling musty and shut-up. The word is often pronounced fiesty or fysty. Lord Berners perhaps gives a clue to its origin when in 1546, referring to a cask as a foist (from Old French *fuste*, a log or piece of timber), he writes that "Good wyne sometyme savoureth of the foyst".

Forelow. A horse standing in an unfavourable position, with his wallis lower than his rump, would be said to be standing forelow; a posture in which no judicious seller would allow him to be exhibited, says Moor.

"Old Fitz" and his sea words

Edward FitzGerald is well known as an Oriental scholar and particularly as the translator of the Rubaiyat of Omar Khayam, but as a Suffolk man he was also keenly interested in the local dialect. "Old Fitz", as he was familiarly and affectionately known in Suffolk, made his contribution to dialect study with "Sea Words and Phrases along the Suffolk Coast", which he sent to the *East Anglian, or Notes and Queries*, in 1869. He followed up with a further article in the same periodical entitled "A Capful of Sea Slang".

Four-releet. A crossroads at which two roads intersect. Where one road meets another without crossing it is a three-releet. It derives from the Anglo-Saxon *wega gelæte*, a road junction, and is sometimes rendered as four-way-leet.

Foxtail. Mare's-tail (*Hippuris vulgaris*), a primitive plant of streams and wet places. See also **Cat's-tail**.

Frawn. A word used in Suffolk for frozen. Moor gives the example "I'm frawn ta dead amost".

Freemartin. A barren heifer that is one of a pair of twins of different sexes. "It is generally known in Suffolk that the martin will not breed—both of a sex prove fertile," says Moor.

French spink. The brambling. The word spink is derived from the bird's call note.

Fresher. A young frog.

Fulfer. Probably a variant pronunciation of fieldfare, a winter visitor, but also used for the resident mistle thrush. Indeed, the fieldfare was sometimes known as a French fulfer, in contradistinction to the English fulfer or mistle thrush.

Furrow-chuck. The whinchat.

Fuzhacker. The stonechat and whinchat. A combination of furze and hacker or stutterer, a word of Saxon origin.

Fye out. To clean out, or clear out, a room, a cupboard, a ditch, etc. See **Bottom-fying**.

Game hawk. The peregrine, which the Rev Richard Lubbock records as having bred on the spire of Norwich Cathedral, "to the great annoyance of the pigeon fanciers of this city".

Gargut root. Bear's-foot (*Helleborus viridus*).

Winter has set in, the snow and ice makes the path slippery, and the woman looks "frawn ta dead."

Garland flower. Mezerion (*Daphne mezereum*), also known in Norfolk as Cornelian.

Garlick. Charlock (*Sinapis arvensis*), once an abundant weed of arable land.

Gatter-bush, gattridge. Guelder-rose (*Viburnum opulus*).

Gatway. A word of Norse origin used for a channel between the coastal sandbanks or across a sandbank. The word is in fact tortological, since in the Norse the word *get* means a way or road. The Cockle Gat between the Cockle Sand and the North Scroby is the northern entrance to Yarmouth Roads, a much-used anchorage in the days of sail, and the St Nicholas Gat across the

The Rev Robert Forby and
The Vocabulary of East Anglia

At about the same time that Major Edward Moor was gathering together a collection of Suffolk words several people were engaged on a similar task in Norfolk. One of them was the Rev William Tylney Spurdens, a native of Suffolk, who with a friend, John Deere of Brundall, had begun a collection of what they called *Icenisms* about 1808.

Spurdens and Deere were no academic collectors of words but did their collecting in the field in the course of their sporting and other activities. It was while visiting St Benet's Abbey, beside the Bure on the marshes south of Ludham, that they discovered the true origin of Sammodithee, a word which had puzzled and misled some very learned antiquaries.

Through Dawson Turner, the Yarmouth antiquary, Deere learnt that the Rev Robert Forby, who was the incumbent of Fincham, near Swaffham, was engaged in compiling a record of "the vulgar tongue" of East Anglia as it had existed in the last twenty years of the eighteenth century. With commendable generosity Spurdens and Deere agreed to make common cause with him.

Born at Stoke Ferry, in West Norfolk, and educated at Lynn, Robert Forby graduated from Caius College, Cambridge, in 1781. He became a Fellow and seemed likely to lead an academic life, but instead became a country parson and, like many impecunious clerics, took private pupils whose fathers were prepared to pay for a classical education. After spending some time at Barton Bendish he moved to Fincham, a more valuable living, in 1801. The study of dialect was not by any means his only interest, for he was a keen botanist, and was in 1798 elected a Fellow of the Linnaean Society.

The book that resulted from the three men's work did not appear until 1830, five years after Forby's sudden death. Another of Forby's collaborators was the Rev George Turner, of Kettleburgh, near Framlingham, and it fell to him to edit the material left by Forby, though he admitted that he was not always able to decipher parts of the manuscript that appeared to have been unfinished at the time of the author's death. Turner seems to have been unaware of the participation of Spurdens and Deere in the gathering of material for Forby's book, and no acknowledgment of their work appeared in the preface of *The Vocabulary of East Anglia*. Among the subscribers was Major Moor.

Some years after the publication of *The Vocabulary of East Anglia* under Forby's name Spurdens, who was then living at North Walsham, produced a manuscript for a supplementary volume. He in his turn died before his work could be published, and it did not appear until 1858.

Spurdens' supplement to *The Vocabulary of East Anglia* was edited by the Rev Walter Skeat and reprinted in the fourth part of the English Dialect Society Reprinted Glossaries in 1879, together with a list of Suffolk words from the second edition of the Rev Sir John Cullum's *The History of Hawsted and Hardwick, in the County of Suffolk*, published in 1813.

Spurdens was not alone in wishing to add to Forby's vocabulary. In 1857 the Rev Greville J. Chester contributed a list of words to *Norfolk Archaeology*, including some words from the John Steele manuscript in the Bodleian Library, and in 1879 William Waters, of Hindringham, contributed a further list to the same publication.

northern end of the Corton Sand provided an approach for small vessels to the harbour entrance at Gorleston. Off the Essex coast is Goldmer Gat, lying between the West Rocks off Harwich and the north-eastern end of the Gunfleet Sand and forming the northern entrance to the Wallet.

Those street-names ending in -gate often have the same Norse origin, and in such cases do not refer to a town gate. Examples are Pottergate, Westlegate and Finkelgate in Norwich, Blyburgate and Northgate in Beccles and, by way of comparison, Sandgate in Trondheim.

Gavel. A sheaf of corn before it is tied up, says Forby. Besides being used as a noun the word was employed as a verb, to collect mown corn into heaps; Major Moor, as usual, described the operation in some detail. "To gather mown barley, or oats, or hay, with hand-rakes into rows and small loose cocks, ready to pitch on to the waggon. The persons, generally women, who do this are called gavellers, and the corn in such rows is said to lie on the gavel, or in gavels." Arthur Young in his *General View of the Agriculture of the County of Suffolk* (1813) writes of cole-seed being "reaped, and left on the gravel till fit to thresh"; perhaps the compositor misread *gavel* as *gravel.*

Gawp. To gape very wide, as Forby says; to stare with a sort of idiotic wonder. In Holland the chemist's shops all have a sign of a head with mouth wide open and tongue protruding, known as a Gaaper; in modern Dutch *gaapen* is to yawn.

Generals. Always used in the plural, this was the name commonly used in the Diocese of Norwich for the Archdeacon's Visitation. Until the formation of the Diocese of St Edmundsbury and Ipswich in 1914 the Norwich Diocese, one of the biggest in the country, included all of Suffolk as well as the county of Norfolk. Forby, who said that the Norwich Diocese seemed to be the only one in which this popular name was used,

suggested that it arose from the Visitation being officially called the Archdeacon's General Court.

Gimmers, jimmers. Small hinges such as those on furniture, or sometimes a door hinge. Both Forby and Moor include this word, but it is apparent that its use was not confined to East Anglia.

Gladdon. The Norfolk name for lesser reedmace (*Typha augustifolia*) and yellow flag (*Iris pseudacorus*), cut on the Broads for the making of horse collars and frail baskets. Both, as Ted Ellis explains, are plants with sword-shaped leaves, from *gladius*, a sword.

Gleave. Fenland word for an eel spear. See also **Eel pick.**

Goaf or goof. A stack of corn in the straw laid up in a barn. Moor adds the information that "riding the goof" was the work of a boy on horseback to compress the corn as it was thrown on to the goof. Such a horse, according to Spurdens, was known as a goaf-horse; "usually ridden by a boy: an elevation not to be envied", he added. The plural is goaves. The goaf-stead was the division of a barn in which a goaf was placed; a large barn might have four or more. The threshing floor was called the middle-stead.

Goaf-flap. A wooden beater used in Norfolk to knock up the ends of the sheaves to make the goaf or stack more compact. Forby declares that such a device was seldom if ever used in Suffolk, but it was a standing joke on 1st April to send a boy to borrow a goaf-flap; "and the messenger invariably runs the gauntlet of all the servants and labourers at the farm house, to which he is sent," Forby adds. In a later age it was common to send apprentices to a shop for "a box of rubber tintacks" or for "a ha'porth of strap oil"; in the latter case the shopkeeper was expected to remove his leather belt from around his waist and administer the required "strap-oil".

Goatsucker. The nightjar, which in the Rev Richard Lubbock's *Observations on the Fauna of Norfolk* (1845) is referred to only by the name goatsucker. See also **Buzzhawk**, **Dorhawk**.

Goave. To stow corn in a barn. As an example of the use of this verb Forby gives the quotation "do you intend to stack this wheat [in the open], or to goave it?" Tusser uses the word:

In goving at harvest learn skilfully how
Each grain for to lay by itself on the mow:
Seed barley the purest gove out of the way,
All other nigh hand, gove just as ye may.

Tusser also mentions a gofe-ladder used to reach the top of the goaf; and Moor remarks that in his time the ladder so used was still called a goaf-ladder.

Godsgood. Yeast. Forby renders the word *Gosgood* and ridicules the suggestion by John Ray (1674) that it was originally God's good; John Steele's manuscript of about 1712, however, does indeed render it *Godsgood*, and the *Oxford English Dictionary* seems to confirm this origin of the word. To begin with, God's good was anything that was seen as the good gift of God; the self-perpetuating nature of yeast no doubt made it seem very much a gift of God. The word was, says Forby, "utterly extinct" in his time (c.1820); "the taste remains," he adds.

The season for cutting gladdon came directly after harvest, as the leaves began to turn yellow. Cutting was done from a boat, using a meak, and the bundles of bolder were then carted home in the boat.

The grammar of East Anglia

East Anglian dialect has its own grammar, quite different from the English grammar that used to be taught in schools. Schoolteachers for the most part tended to regard regional variations in grammar as careless or mistaken use of English, but these variations can all be traced back to particular influences. Not only do many dialect variations stem from a form of English that was spoken in Chaucer's time, but has since changed, but instances of similar variations can be found in certain foreign languages that provide clues to the origin of East Anglian dialect.

The separable prefix that is so striking a feature of our dialect is found also in Dutch and German, and is likely to have been introduced to East Anglia by incoming travellers who settled on the East Coast perhaps a thousand years ago. As in German, so do we tell someone "Push the door to!", and as the door is opened by somebody else, we might ask "Where are you a-going to?" The latter is similar to the Cumbrian "Where's ta gang til?", supposedly a survival of Danish or Swedish speech introduced by Viking invaders.

The double demonstrative "that there" is certainly of Scandinavian origin. Often used by speakers of East Anglian dialect, it is considered incorrect English; it is popular Danish, and correct Swedish.

Then there is the double negative that has proved a challenge to generations of schoolteachers in Norfolk and Suffolk; it was once common in many languages, including everyday English. The countryman who is heard to say that "he hin't seen naathin'" is making use of a form of speech that has passed out of use in ordinary English, yet still survives in Afrikaans, a derivative of the Dutch language spoken in South Africa.

The peculiar half-cough given by a Norfolk man instead of the "T" in words such as butter and water seems comparable with the "glottal stop" of Danish speech, and is probably a survival of it. There is a well-known story of the schoolteacher who had great difficulty in making little Tommy sound the "T" in the word butter; when at last he managed to stutter out something akin to what she considered the right pronunciation she burst out, greatly relieved, "Good, Tommy, thass be'er!"

Gon, gun. The past participle of to give, more normally gave. "I gon it to him yisterday."

Good few, a. Rather more than a few, quite a lot.

Goose tansey. Silverweed (*Potentilla anserina*), a common native plant of waste ground, roadsides and damp meadows.

Gotch-belly. A good round belly much resembling the shape of a gotch, an earthenware jug of a very rounded form.

Go-to-bed-at-noon, John-go-to-bed-at-noon. The Goat's-beard (*Tragopogon pratensis*), whose flowers open in the morning but close again before dinnertime.

Go-to-meeting clothes. One's Sunday suit, best clothes. While the churchman attended service, the Nonconformist went to his meeting.

Gowden-bug. The ladybird or bishabarn-abee. The Suffolk pronunciation of the word golden might be thought a mere error, but it

Gun punt is not dialect, just a descriptive term for a punt mounting a long-barrelled gun with which wildfowlers went in search of waterfowl. In this photograph from Life and Landscape on the Norfolk Broads *the fowler has returned to his boathouse, a rough structure of wood and thatch.*

is perhaps significant that the Dutch word is indeed *gouden*. See **Bishabarnabee**.

Grass-weed. Fennel-leaved pondweed (*Potomogeton pectinatus*).

Grass widow. Never mind the modern definition; Forby defines the expression uncompromisingly as "a forsaken fair one, whose nuptials, not celebrated in a church, were consummated, in all pastoral simplicity, on the green turf". The parish register of Stoke-by-Nayland contains an entry for 1582, "Jan., The 31 day was bur'ed Marie the daught[r] of Elizabeth London graswidow". The present-day meaning of a wife whose husband is absent on business (or on the golf course) seems to have originated in India, where wives spent the hot weather in the hills while their menfolk went about their business at a lower, infinitely less comfortable, altitude.

Green ulf. The greenfinch, otherwise known in Suffolk as a green linnet, in contradistinction to the red linnet, the true linnet, which I have seen referred to as the grey linnet, a reference to its grey head.

Green weed. The Dyer's broom (*Genista tinctoria*), a native plant that was once cultivated as a source of dye but is now rarely found.

Grey parson, Grey-coat parson. A layman who hired the tithes of the parson, according to the Rev Sir John Cullum of Hawsted. A tithe was a tax of one-tenth of the annual produce of land or labour, levied to support the clergy and the Church.

Grigg. A large willow basketwork eel trap used in the Fens. Unlike the hive, it was not baited.

Grindle. A small, narrow stream or drain; there is a stream at Stanton in Suffolk known as The Grindle, and a similarly named one at Chelmondiston which reaches the Orwell at the well-known hamlet of Pin Mill. Also known in Suffolk as a drindle, which Forby notes as "a very neat diminutive of drain".

Grounds. Individual fields on washland, a term used in the Fens. Phil Gray in his delightful book *The Washlanders* gives an example of its usage: "Holland's bullocks are three grounds down from Jacobs' Hovels," the latter being old milking sheds on the Nene Washes near Whittlesey.

Grup. In modern usage the drain leading from the edge of the road into the roadside ditch to clear water from the road. However, Forby defines it as "a trench, not amounting in breadth to a ditch. If narrower still, it is a grip; if extremely narrow, a gripple". There appears to be a Scandinavian origin; in Faeroese *gropa* is to dig a hole. An associated word is **grooping**, the cutting of a groove, as in coopering; the cooper used his **grooping-iron** to make the groove around the inside of the barrel to receive the head.

Guleham. The yellowhammer, possibly from the Norse *gul* for yellow.

Gull. A miniature ravine cut by a fast-flowing stream. There is a public house at Framingham Earl, between Norwich and Loddon, whose sign shows a seagull; it was actually named after the nearby drainage channel. Forby defines gull as a verb meaning to sweep away by force of running water and also as "a breach or hole made by the force of a torrent". It is presumably related to gully and gully-hole, the mouth of a street drain or of any other kind of drain for that matter. In the Fens the same term is used for a horseshoe-shaped bend in a river where the banks have been repaired after a breach, this use of the term reflecting Forby's definition.

Hain, to. To raise or heighten. When patent sails replaced the old canvas sails on the marsh mills of the Broads region some of the brick towers were hained by building a vertical section on top of the tower. In other circumstances it might be said that a worker had "hed his wages hained". The word is derived from the Anglo-Saxon *heign*, to heighten.

Hair-weed. Fennel-leaved pondweed (*Potamogeton pectinatus*).

Hake. An iron hook on which the pot hung over the kitchen fire, from Old Norse *haki*, Middle Dutch *hake* and modern Dutch *haak*. The hakes hung from the gallow-balk, a strong iron bar fixed in the chimney. Spurdens says of the word hake "this is now chiefly used for a kind of gate which swings over the kitchen fire, or another utensil which hangs down the chimney, both used for suspending pots and boilers", suggesting that the word hake had been transferred to the gallow-balk or what in common parlance was a fire crane. Somebody who has got very dirty indeed is "as black as the hakes".

Ham. A small bay or inlet. Leathes Ham at Oulton is a good example, though it was separated from Lake Lothing when the railway embankment was built across it in 1846. The word is much used of inlets on the broads, but it is also used on the coast.

Hansel. The first money taken by a tradesman in the day. The tradesman was apt to spit on it "for luck" before pocketing it.

Ha'pennies-and-pennies. Frogbit (*Hydrocharis morsus-ranae*).

Harnser. A heron, an old name that was well known to Shakespeare: in *Hamlet* a character says "I know a hawk from a handsaw", a sentence that has puzzled many a schoolboy down the years. In 1766 Pennant wrote that "Not to know the Hawk from the Heron-shaw, was an old proverb taken from this diversion [heron-hawking]; but in course of time, served to express great ignorance in any science". Forby spells the word harnsey, but remembering the Norfolk habit of changing a *y* sound into an *a* as in dicka it is perhaps better spelt as we have done. It is in origin not a dialect word at all but a contraction of the old word heronsew or heronshaw, a diminutive of heron. In the Squire's Tale Geoffrey Chaucer wrote "I wal not tellen. . . of hir swannes nor of hir heronsewes". Whether you call him a heron or a harnser, the grey heron, a bird which is increasing in number on the Broads, knows his own name, which he announces as he flaps away, "Fraank!"

Harnser-gutted. Lanky and lean, like the heron.

Harry-carry. A Yarmouth troll-cart. See **Trolly**.

Hassocks. Tussock sedge (*Carex paniculata* and *C. appropinquata*), a typical plant of the Broadland. Such tussocks were sometimes cut and used as kneelers, or hassocks, in parish churches.

Hayjack. The whitethroat.

Hedge-betty. A hedge-sparrow or dunnock. Anyone who has watched a dunnock seeking food on a shady country path, darting here and there and back again, will appreciate the significance of this name. See **betty about**.

A Yarmouth troll-cart or harry-carry on the beach, waiting for swills of herring landed from fishing luggers lying offshore.

Hen's nose. A hen's noseful is an expressive way of describing something very small indeed. A small fire in the grate has been described as "a little owd hen's nose of a fire". When the compiler was a boy he learnt an odd rhyme:

> Once upon a time, when pigs drank wine,
>   The monkeys chewed tobacco;
> The hens took snuff, to make them tough,
>   And the ducks cried "What's the matter?"

Herb Tuppence. Creeping Jenny (*Lysimachia nummularia*), a native plant of wet meadows and ditches.

Het. Past participle of the verb *To heat*. The Rev F. Barham Zincke notes the use of this old strong participle in his *Some Materials for the History of Wherstead* (1887). Today someone who is getting angry will still be told "Don't get het up".

Higgler. An itinerant dealer in small wares, says Moor. In this sense the word is by no means confined to East Anglia, and one wonders if the word is derived from one who haggles, that is one who tries to beat down the price he pays for a commodity, by way of the familiar East Anglian change of vowel. Forby describes the verb higgle as "to be nice and tedious in bargaining", and further describes it as a diminutive of haggle, with a sense of contempt, implying the most petty chaffering.

Forby also mentions a second meaning, to effect by slow degrees and by minute sparing and saving. The poor, he says, often talked of "higgling up a pig", buying it and fattening it up on scraps. It is perhaps not without significance that one use of the word higgler was for a person who bought poultry to fatten for market.

Highlows. A covering for the foot and ankle, too high to be called a shoe and too low for a boot, says Forby. Major Moor adds that they are tightly laced in front, midleg high, with a thong or lace known in Suffolk as a whang. A correspondent in the *Eastern Daily Press* some years ago stated that the original highlows were eighteenth-century military boots, mentioned as such in Thackeray's novel *The Virginians*. The word is often quoted as a dialect word, but it has a much wider usage.

Hinder. Yonder, often used in the sense of something moving or coming up from a distance. As an instance of that usage, Claxton quotes "He oon't be long afore he's here, hinder he come."

Hinny. The offspring of a donkey by a stallion. It is smaller and less robust than a mule, which is the offspring of a mare by a donkey.

His, hers, mine, ours, theirs, yours. Used in the sense of home, as in "He come round to mine last night, and I went back to his".

Hive. A Fenland eel trap made of willow, basket fashion. It was usually baited. See also **Grigg**.

Hobby. A pony or a small horse, an old word which survived only in the dialect. It seems likely to be derived from the name Hobin, Hobby, a variation of Robin and Robbie; a writer in 1695 observed that "our ploughmen to some one of their cart-horses generally give the name Hobin". A variation of this name is Dobbin, which in general usage became a generic name for a carthorse.

Hobby lantern. A will-o'-the-wisp or Jack-a-lantern; Forby spells it the old way, hobby lanthorn, and seeks to explain the term by pointing to the motion of a will-o'-the-wisp, "as if it were a lanthorn ambling and curvetting on the back of a hobby".

Hodmedod. A snail. When a girl's hair is done up in curl papers or rags, she is said to have her hodmedods in, or to have her hair in hodmedods. Bacon in *Sylva* (1626) wrote of animals "that cast their Shell, are: The

Lobster, the Crab, the Crafish, the Hodman-dod or Dodman, the Tortoise". See also **Dodman**.

Hogweed. Not the true hogweed (*Heracleum sphondylium*), locally known as cow parsnip or cow mumble, or its giant counterpart (*H. mantegazzianum*) but Knotgrass (*Polygonum aviculare*), a common weed of arable and waste ground.

Shocking corn, a photograph from P.H. Emerson's Pictures of East Anglian Life. *The harvest was the culmination of the farming year, and the horkey was the farmworker's great celebration.*

Holler, to. To shout. It is no more than the verb to hollo, hollow or holla, meaning to cry out loud, to shout, which has passed out of common usage except in the hunting field.

At harvest time a boy would ride astride the leading horse of the team hauling the waggon and would holler "howdye!", a warning to those on the waggon that the team was about to move. In effect it was similar to the bus conductor's cry of "Hold tight!" as he rang the bell telling the driver to set off; with the onset of one-man operation of buses even this phrase has become just a memory.

Home Fishing. The East Anglian autumn herring voyage.

Horkey. A harvest-home feast or frolic. In J. Gage's *History and Antiquities of Hengrave, in Suffolk*, published in 1822, there is a pleasant account of what he calls the "hockay", which was even then becoming a thing of the past. "The custom after harvest of crying largess prevails generally among the people in this neighbourhood; but the hockay, or harvest-home, since the introduction of task-work at the reaping season, begins to fall into disuse. When this good old custom is kept here with due solemnity, besides the usual homage paid to the master and mistress of the house, a ceremony takes place which affords much mirth: a pair of ram's-horns, painted and decorated with flowers, is carried in triumph round the festive board; and as the forester who had killed the deer was honored of old with the buck's horns and saluted with a ditty (*As you Like it*, IV.2.) so the harvest-man of Hengrave having finished his labours is crowned with the ram's-horns, and greeted with a song which has the same point as the other, though more coarsely expressed."

Edward Moor in 1823 recalled that flip, a potation compounded of beer, gin and coarse sugar, used to be the principal ingredient in the festivities, but "it is to be lamented that, since gentlemen have turned farmers, and farmers have turned gentlemen (a transformation that both perhaps begin to repent) these scenes of jollity and merriment have in too many cases been shifted from the farm-house to the ale-house: and have consequently degenerated from harmless happiness to debauchery and mischief".

Curiously Moor seemed to consider hockey or horkey a Norfolk word, but in his supplement to Forby the Rev W.T. Spurdens says the word was chiefly used in High Suffolk. Forby spells it Hawkey, suggesting that the word could be derived from hark ye—to the festive call, the voice of joy and revelry, he explains. And he adds that "an ingenious lady proposed the French words *haut cri*, as a derivation. Very descriptive, but more plausible than probable."

Forby goes on to tell how the Hawkey-load, the last load of the crop, was always in former times led home on the evening of the hawkey, with much rustic pageantry; the load and the horses were decorated with flags, streamers and garlands, and attended by a troop of masquers in grotesque disguises.

Hornpie. The lapwing or green plover.

Horrywaur. Edward FitzGerald included this entry in his "Sea Words and Phrases along the Suffolk Coast", published in *The East Anglian, or Notes and Queries*, in 1869, and prefaced his note with "Fifty pounds to the philologer who will guess this riddle without looking to the end for its solution." One cannot resist reproducing his note verbatim, because Old Fitz's own words are not to be satisfactorily paraphrased.

"When first I knew Lowestoft, some forty years ago [c.1830], the herring luggers (which then lay up on the beach, when not at sea), very many of them bore testimony to Wesley's visits to the place, and his influence on the people. Beside the common family and familiar names, such as the William, Sarah Jane, Two Friends, Brothers, and such like; there were the Ebenezer, Barzillai, Salem, and many more Old Testament names; beside the Faith, Hope, Charity, &c., from later Revelation. A few vessels bore names in profane story—such as the Shannon (which, by-the-by, still *reigns*) after Sir Philip Broke's victory; there was even a William Tell (no longer reigning), whose effigies, drest in an English sailor's white ducks and blue jacket, pointed at the wind with a pistol from the mast-head. *That* was about the furthest reach of legendary or historical lore. But *now* the schoolmaster has been at sea, as well as abroad, and gone herring-driving—Bless me! there's now a Nil Desperandum, a Dum Spiro Spero, and last, not least, a Meum and Tuum; though in the latter case it was very properly represented to the owners that the phrase being Latin, should properly run Meum *et* Tuum. Then even the detested *Parley-vous* has come into request; and you may hear of a *scrunk* of luggers very gravely enumerated in such order as the following. 'Let me see, there was the Young William, the Chanticleer, the Quee Vive (Qui Vive), the Saucy Polly, the Hosanna, and the Horrywaur!' Of the latter I could get no explanation, until one day it flashed upon me when I saw sailing out among the fleet, the Au Revoir, belonging to a very good fellow who (according to the custom of nicknames hereabout) goes, as I believe his father went before him, under the name of *Dickymilk*."

Hover. A floating island of reed broken away from a reedbed by storm-force winds. Many of the reedbeds surrounding broads are little more than floating mattresses, and it is not difficult for a storm to wrench a section free; on one occasion a huge hover from the south side of Heigham Sounds drifted down-river and blocked Potter Heigham bridge. Spurdens notes the word hovvers or huvvers, meaning dried flags used as fuel. Whereas turves were blocks of peat taken from beneath the surface, hovvers were pared from the surface and one face was made up of grass and sedge.

The Horse and the Dialect

DURING the thousand years or so that the East Anglian dialect was taking form and in use the primary source of power and transport both on the farm and in towns was the horse. Much dialect speech, therefore, had to do with the horse, with its use and with its care.

Suffolk, of course, has its own breed of horse, short of leg and barrel chested. The Rev Sir John Cullum mentions their virtues in his history of Hawsted (1784): "The breed is well known by the name of Suffolk Punches. They are generally about fifteen hands high, of a remarkably short and compact make; their legs bony and their shoulders loaded with flesh. Their colour is often of a light sorrel, which is as much remembered in some distant parts of the kingdom as their form. They are not made to indulge the rapid impatience of this posting generation; but for draught they are perhaps unrivalled as for their gentle and tractable temper . . . With wonder and gratitude have I seen them with the most spirited executions unsolicited by the whip, and indignant as it were at the obstacles that opposed them, drawing my carriage up the rocky and precipitous roads of Denbigh and Caernarvonshire."

Suffolk Punches are, it has to be said, thought of today more as farm horses than as coach horses. The breed as known today can be traced back to a single stallion, Crisp's Horse of Ufford, descended from the old breed of Suffolks known to Sir John.

Colts had to be broken in, a process known in Norfolk as cowt breearking. A correspondent from Saxlingham described this in a letter to the *Eastern Daily Press* in 1949 in the following terms: "Arter they ha' put the halter on neatly, the collar go on wi' trace over the back; then dutphin with bit to suit nature of mouth (hard or sorft), to which is fastened a rope either side.

"A man walk on each side and one behind. The man behind spar the cowt forward by such words as 'gurup' (get up, or go forward). Then the cowt have to carcle so many times to the left, the man with that line repeating 'cubbear' (come here). Then carcling right, the man on that side repeating 'whoish'.

"The time come when broken enough to hitch 'em to the plough. Then is seen if they have been good pupils. If not you hear the man at the plough say 'cubbear—whoish—gurup', and if the cowt answer the call 'cubbear' too smart, I have heard 'cubbear whoish' at the same time, and if wanted to stop 'weaase' (whoa)."

The words indicating direction varied somewhat according to the district. Forby gives Hait-wo as the word of command to a team to go left, pointing out that Chaucer used the word heit in the same way. In some areas it was cubbear to turn left, in others come-hither or even come-harley, the suggestion being that a man leading a horse walked on the left of the horse's head and so in effect called the horse to him when he wanted it to turn left. William Waters, who hailed from Hindringham, in 1879 recorded that the command as he knew it was harley-harther. Whoish, weirsh, weesh are variations of the command to turn right, which some have sought to derive from the French word gauche—left!

In Norfolk a team of four horses would be led by the fore-horse, next being the lash-horse, then the pin-horse and, between the shafts, the shaft-horse. The last-named was at one time known as the thill-horse, but William Waters in 1879 said that the term was at that time quite obsolete, though auctioneers' catalogues still spoke of thill-horse gears.

Terms for parts of the harness also varied from place to place. In Norfolk the wooden (or metal) fittings on a horse's collar were the hames, in Suffolk they were known as seles. To them were hooked the traise, the tug-chains linking the collar to the shafts or to the implement being used.

How, fare so. Awkward, as in "trouble with him, he fare so how".

Hubgrubbing. A very descriptive word meaning dirty, piggish. There is a story of a farmworker watching pigs at the trough who commented, "Dutty things, no wonder they call 'em pigs!"

Hulver. The holly. The word appears to be derived from the Old Norse *hulfr* by way of late Middle English *hulfere*. Around the village of Hulver, a few miles east of Beccles, there grow many holly bushes in the hedgerows.

Hull, to. To throw, presumably a variation of hurl. James Spillings tells of a man who went into a chemist's shop in North Norfolk and asked for "a punno' o' pills to hull a wummen into a sweat".

Indoor servant. A servant in the country who was employed entirely within doors and not in the fields or the garden. A somewhat similar position was occupied by an inward-maid, the housemaid in a farmhouse who was not expected to work in the dairy.

Iron-sided dog. A boy who fears nobody, and plays all sorts of mischievous tricks.

Jag. A waggon load, particularly of hay, straw or corn in the straw. In Sir John Cullum's pioneering history of Hawsted one finds: "Sept. 1700.— Carried the widow Smith one jagg of thorns, 0£ 12s.0d." Moor says that the word is applied only to a waggon load, not to a cart load or to the load carried on a man's back, but Forby on the other hand defines a jag as "an indefinite quantity, but less than a load, of hay or corn in the straw." Claxton, writing in the 1950s, goes further: "A small load, less than a tumbril load, of hay, straw or wood."

Jim or jill. A two-wheeled vehicle used to transport heavy logs. It has a single shaft fitted to the top of the arched member which links the two wheels; the shaft is allowed to become upright and the log is chained to the arched member; the shaft is then hauled down and fastened to the log, this operation raising the log clear of the ground so that it can be transported. Moor comments that while jim was in universal use in Suffolk the word jill was used in Norfolk, where a drug was called a timber-jack.

Job. A piece of work taken at a fixed or stated price, and which a labourer would finish at his own pace. Both Sir John Cullum of Hawsted and Major Moor refer to "working by the job", and the latter adds that job and jobben were also used in the sense of striking or pecking. Fowls or birds job at anything hard, as did a man picking up a road with a mattock or pick. Moor comments that jub, or jubbing, would also be applied to the operation of using a pick, especially if lazily done, by the day.

Joskin. With the expansion of the herring fishery in the nineteenth century many farmworkers from coastal areas of Norfolk and Suffolk went to sea in the luggers as capstan hands; their job was to walk round and round the old-fashioned capstan hauling in the warp. These men were known

A timber jim at Lowestoft, hauled behind a horse-drawn trolley.

to other fishermen as joskins, which is explained in the *Oxford English Dictionary* as merely a slang word for a countryman. The Home Fishing, the autumn herring voyage, came conveniently for them after harvest and at a slack period on the farm. Some joskins did very well at a time when there was good money to be made from the fishing, and not a few continued to go to sea in the drifters even after Elliott and Garrood of Beccles had introduced their steam capstan; a few even rose to command the drifters in which they sailed.

Journey. Or as Major Moor spells it, phonetically, jahney. A day's work. "One jahney" is when the horses do their whole day's ploughing at once; "tew jahneys" is leaving off work about noon and resuming it at about two o'clock, Moor tells us.

Nathaniel Kent in his *General View of the Agriculture of the County of Norfolk* (1796) tells how "instead of working them [the horses] seven hours in winter and eight in summer, as they do in most other counties, without drawing their bits, they are worked eight hours in winter and ten in summer, by two journies as they are termed, which enable them to do considerably more than they would by one journey . . . besides, the heat in summer is more avoided by this means".

"Two journies a day used to be the good practice of Suffolk husbandry—but in these times when 'more pay and less work' is the 'universal toast' it is nearly obsolete," says Moor, writing in 1823. "During the war [the Napoleonic Wars] the scarcity of labourers resulting from, or increased by, the high price of agricultural produce, rendered servants rather dainty; and 'tew jahnies' was objected to by many. The cause has ceased, but not the effect; and the day's work now, summer as well as winter, usually is from ½-past 7 to ½-past 2."

In contradiction of Major Moor's suggestion that Suffolk workers used to go two journeys, George Ewart Evans shows in *The Horse in the Furrow* that one journey was a

survival from the era when teams of four or eight oxen were used in ploughing the fields. The amount of time and trouble involved in yoking and unyoking a team of oxen, to say nothing of the distance between stables and field, made it natural that ploughing should be done in one extended visit to the field.

The origin of the word journey is to be found in the use by medieval monks of the Latin word *jurnalis* (or *diurnalis*) for the acre or strip which was the average day's ploughing for an ox-team.

Kedge, kidge, kedgy. Brisk, hale and hearty, in good spirits. Both Moor and Forby record the word, the latter saying that it is applied almost exclusively to hale and cheerful old people. The origin is obscure, but it was certainly in use in the same sense as jolly in the fifteenth century.

Keeler. A tub, usually made by a cooper, used for a variety of purposes. A wherry carried a "hand-killer", a small wooden handbasin, square in form, which was normally kept under the sternsheets and filled from the river.

Kentishman. A hooded crow (*Corvus corone cornix*), once a more common winter visitor to East Anglia than it is now. Arthur Patterson remarks in *Nature in Eastern Norfolk* (1905) that "it performs a useful office in devouring carrion, a continual and abundant supply of which is always to be discovered in the vicinity of tidal waters", but goes on to add that "in severe winters the Hooded Crow certainly shows its predatory instincts, and will not only seize upon wounded fowl, but even snap up small birds in the very presence of the gunner".

Kid, to. Edward FitzGerald tells us that this was to signal how many herrings were on board a lugger. "The arm struck forward signifies a last; waved round, a thousand," he says.

King-cup. The marsh marigold (*Caltha palustris*).

King George. The peacock butterfly.

King Harry. A goldfinch. Perhaps a folk-memory of the splendid attire of King Henry VIII led to this name being given to what is, after all, one of our most resplendent little birds. More likely, however, is the explanation that the name comes from the Norse *hæren*, meaning an army; a reference to the goldfinches' habit of going about in small flocks in search of seeds. Also known as a **draw-water**.

Lace-weed. Fennel-leaved pondweed (*Potomogeton pectinatus*).

Lamb's skin. Floating sheets of algae whose filaments form a skin on the surface of the water.

Lantern men. Will-o'-the-wisps, caused by spontaneous combustion of marsh gas (methane). Nevertheless, no such down-to-earth explanation would satisfy old-time marshmen, who believed them to be supernatural and far more dangerous, and had many a story to bear out their belief. See also **Hobby lantern**.

Last. A measure of herring used in the East Anglian herring fishery until the introduction of the cran measure. The fish were counted by taking two in each hand, the four herrings making a warp; thirty-three warps

A fish auction on Yarmouth beach at a time when herring was sold by the last, nominally 10,000 fish but when counted out actually 13,200.

(132 fish) went to a hundred (a long hundred, that is), and a hundred hundred (13,200 fish) made a last. Nall tells us that when computed by measurement, rather than by counting, twenty swills (the odd baskets used at Yarmouth for handling herring) were computed to form a last. The word is probably derived from the Anglo-Saxon *hlæst*, a load. An even older measure was the cade, which contained six hundred (792 fish). It appears to have been adopted from a Norman French term for a barrel holding that number of fish. FitzGerald recorded that in the 1860s Aldeburgh fishermen still spoke of a cade of sprats, 1,000 fish.

Laughing goose. The white-fronted goose, so called from its call.

Ligger. A plank laid across a dyke as a footbridge. That legendary Norfolk keeper Jim Vincent had a way of getting his own back on those people who did not do as he told them when out shooting on the Hickling estate. As they made their way back after the evening flight they would have to cross a ligger over a muddy dyke, and his lordship would complain he could not see where to put his feet; Jim, who had already crossed, would stand in the middle of the ligger facing his lordship and strike several matches to show him the way over. As his lordship slowly shuffled across the ligger Jim would say he was sorry, he had no more matches. Blinded by the matches that had been struck, and now in total darkness, his lordship inevitably fell off into the dyke, from which he crawled "smelling something terrible".

Ligger. The same word was also used for a device used for catching pike, generally known as a trimmer. This is a short piece of round wood with a length of fishing line attached, weighted and hooked. The line is wrapped around the stick, leaving some three feet loose. The hook is baited and the device put into the river or broad; if a pike or eel takes the bait the line runs off the stick. On the broads a ligger was often made from a bundle of reeds or rushes.

Lijahs. Small straps worn just below the knees to hold up the trouser legs. These were an essential part of the worker's clothing when trousers were made of heavy, stiff material in order to give his legs freedom of movement.

Links. Sausages, "from being so formed and hung up chain-like when first made," says Moor. "We call two together a latch of links," adds Forby.

London Road. The Milky Way. The Rev F. Barham Zincke in his *Some Materials for the History of Wherstead* (1887) recalls how on a clear starlight night he said something to a farmworker about the Milky Way. "We don't call it by that name," the labourer told him. "We call it the London Road.

"Its name is the London Road because it is the light of the lamps of the carriages and wagons that are travelling to and from London." Today the London Road south of Ipswich is so well lit, with so much motor traffic on it, that one cannot even see the Milky Way.

Loon. The great crested grebe, a common bird of inland waters that breeds on nearly every broad. Happily, the words of the Rev Richard Lubbock, written in the 1840s, have not been borne out: "It will not happen in our time, but perhaps the next generation may speak of this bird, as we now do of bustards, in the past tense. It is sometimes shot for the sake of its feathers, sometimes as pernicious to fish. The eggs are always taken when found; I have known thirty or forty collected from one broad. Surely there are common fish enough in our extensive waters, and a few might be spared for this bird—the greatest ornament of the Norfolk broads."

Lope, to. The verb to lope means to run, from the Dutch *lopen*, to walk. "There he go lopen down the street," might be said of long-legged person in a hurry.

Lowance, lowans or allowance. The beer allowed in harvest work and haymaking, as William and Hugh Raynbird explain in *On the Agriculture of Suffolk* (1849). Trailing-beer was a sum of money given to labourers during or before the haysel by anyone who has passed or is passing over the growing grass, as it makes the crop in that part more difficult to mow, "commonly asked and given in reference to the desired preservation of such partridges' nests as may be met with scythe in hand," the Raynbirds further explain.

To Major Moor a lowans was an item put into a bricklayer's or carpenter's bill of so much in the pound in lieu of beer to his workmen, "tho' probably the job has been lengthened out to the greatest possible extent in view to the four meals a day which the procrastinating knaves look for in 'indoor' work," he adds. The old soldier seems to have suffered much at the hands of such tradesmen, to judge from his sometimes caustic remarks.

In the records of the Caister Company of Beachmen are several entries, "lowans for the cat", presumably evidence that a cat was kept at the company's "shod" to deal with rats and mice.

Lucam, lucomb. A dormer window, or the projecting hoist of a water mill, steam mill or malting by which the sacks of grain were hoisted to the garner floor or bin floor. The *Oxford English Dictionary* has lucarne, and suggests an origin from the French, but the East Anglian lucam seems more likely to have been derived from Dutch, in which the word *loker* is used for a hole or aperture.

Lunnunners. "We thus distinguish the citizens of our vast metropolis," says Moor. "There is nothing that I can remember farther back, than the contempt (I beg pardon) which I was taught to entertain for the ignorance of the Lunnunners, compared with ourselves, in one particular. It was their preferring long, straight, regularly shaped carrots, to the furcated *cringled*, *skranshlin* diminutive ones, which we (who filled ourselves once or twice every day with the raw article while in season) knew, by the best of all tests, to be so much superior. To see our people pick out ship loads of the well shaped roots, to send to town, rejecting for us, as it were, those above described, so much superior, was a standing joke; and, as I have said, excited both our contempt and pity."

Does the Suffolk country boy of today feel the same contempt for supermarket customers whose carrots are washed, measured, straight and regularly shaped?

Maidenhair grass. Quaking grass (*Briza media*).

Mare's fat. Marsh fleabane (*Pulicaria disenterica*).

Mardle. A small pond suitable for watering cattle, or retting flax. The word can be traced back to the Old French *mardelle*.

Mardle. Can be used either as a verb, to gossip or chat, or as a noun, "we had a rare good ol' mardle, he and I". It has been suggested that it derives from the talking that went on around the retting pit, but in fact in this sense the word is derived from the Old English *moedlan*. Rather oddly, neither Forby nor Moor give mardle in this sense; it appears in Spurdens' supplement to Forby as "a jolly meeting" or "to indulge in such jollity"; Spurdens gives maudle as the verb to gossip, but then adds an example, "Tom and I stood mardling (or maudling) by the stile". E.R. Cooper used the word in the title of his book *Mardles from Suffolk*; in his preface to that book he comments that "since I selected the title I have discovered

A pretty little mawther engaged in the occupation of peeling osiers for the basketmaker.

says "a large sort of basket out of which seed corn is sown by broadcast", while John Greaves Nall tells how a *boat maund* was used to land herrings on the beach at Yarmouth; each maund held about 200 fish. FitzGerald in his *Sea Words and Phrases Along the Suffolk Coast* comments that he always heard it pronounced *maand*, which is close to the modern Dutch.

Mawkin. A scarecrow; or "a dirty, ragged, blowzy wench" as Forby neatly defines it. Mawkin or malkin was a diminutive of the woman's name Matilda or Maud, and as early as the fourteenth century at least was being used to describe a slatternly woman. Chaucer used the word:

> "It wol nat come agayn with outen drede
> Na moore than wol Malkynes maydenhede
> Whan she hath lost it in hir wantownesse".

Mawther. A dialect word for a girl or young woman. It is possibly a variant of the word *mother*, and might be derived from Scandinavian; it is perhaps significant that in some Norwegian dialects *mor* (mother) is used of girls, and of course it was common in East Anglia to address women as "mor".

Meece. The plural of mouse.

Mew-hearted. Faint hearted.

Milkmaid's Path. The Milky Way. "As if the heavenly milkmaid had spilt her pail as she crossed over," commented FitzGerald, who gives this variation in his notes on *Sea Words and Phrases Along the Suffolk Coast.* See also **London Road**.

Millymoller. The fluffy seed of the thistle that drifts on the wind in late summer.

Mitchboard. A short post inserted into the midship tabernacle of a herring lugger to support the lowered foremast while the boat was lying to its nets. In the later steam drifters the mitchboard was a carved board

many people who have lived in the county for years, and some Natyves, who do not know what Mardles are, so it is time something was done about it".

Martin snipe. The green sandpiper.

Maund. A basket, especially the open basket used for sowing seed broadcast and also a basket used for herrings or sprats. The word is Anglo-Saxon, but there is a possibility that it was introduced into the East Anglian dialect from the Dutch; *mand* is still found in Dutch and Flemish. In Coverdale's Bible of 1535 we read "Like as a partrich in a maunde, so is the hert of the proude". Moor

Major Edward Moor

It was a former East India Company Army officer, Major Edward Moor, who produced one of the first books to be published on "provincialisms", and his *Suffolk Words and Phrases; or an attempt to collect the lingual localisms of that county* is still among the best and most readable of such books. He would probably never have produced that book if he had not been removed from his native county to become a cadet in India, where he spent some twenty years, long enough, he said, for him to forget the language of his boyhood.

"I was much struck, on my return, by our provincialisms," he wrote in the preface to his book, published in 1823. "The recurring sound of a long forgotten word produced a sensation similar to the welcome sight of an old friend."

In his retirement Major Moor made his home at Bealings House, Great Bealings, a few miles from Woodbridge, where he used to be visited every Christmas by the FitzGeralds from nearby Bredfield; Edward FitzGerald, the translator of *The Rubaiyat of Omar Khayam*, might well have gained his interest in the Orient from the old soldier, who was one of his boyhood heroes.

The major's book is an entertaining as well as erudite collection of dialect words and usages that reflects well his own character. Many of his entries are quoted in this book not so much because of the words they describe but because of the interesting details contained in those descriptions. Such a case is the entry under Droppen, which is no more than a variant pronunciation of the word dropping; as such it does not really deserve an entry, but it appears because the description he gives of the operation of dropping grains of wheat, peas or beans into the holes made by the dibbles is so fascinating to anyone interested in farming practices of an earlier age.

His book, republished in 1970 by David & Charles, contains a wealth of information on Suffolk life in the early nineteenth century. Dipping into it, the reader soon warms to an author who though of superior social status clearly had a feeling for those who worked on the land. One of his fellow-magistrates complained good-humouredly that he was liable to hold up the weekly court sittings because "you could scarce persuade him of a poor man's guilt".

"Somehow all of us in our corner of Suffolk knew something of him; and so again loved something of him," said Edward FitzGerald of his old friend. "For there was nothing at all about him not to be beloved."

on the roof of the wheelhouse, usually bearing the boat's name, which likewise supported the mast when lowered.

Mocking the Church. According to one of the correspondents in *Broad Norfolk* (1893) the people in his village had an idea that if after the banns of marriage had been read by the parson the couple refused to marry they had to pay a fine for "mocking the Church".

Mole country. The churchyard. The Rev Greville J. Chester in *Norfolk Archaeology*, 1857, gives the example: "He's gone to the mole-country, bless his bones."

Molgogger. A portable fairlead having both vertical and horizontal rollers used in steam drifters. It had a long iron shank which was fitted into holes in the drifter's rail, and the warp, the main rope to which all the nets were made fast, was passed through the

Hauling the nets on board a steam drifter; the warp comes aboard through a molgogger set up on the rail.

rollers when hauling. Because it was portable it was possible to vary the molgogger's position according to prevailing weather and sea conditions. The origin of the molgogger is obscure, but it might have been designed originally for minesweeping in the First World War and copied thereafter by fishermen whose boats had been converted to minesweeping; the origin of the name is even more obscure. Also known as a **Mole-jenny**.

Morphry. A harvest waggon made by adding a fore-carriage with two small wheels to a two-wheeled tumbril or cart. The word morphry is a shortened form of hermaphrodite, an animal or plant having both male and female organs in the same body; hence "neither one thing nor the other", as a countryman might say.

Mort. A great number, as in "a mort of people". Moor sets down an old East Anglian saying, "One is none, tew is some, three is a sort, four is a mort" and adds archly "this may have been current when the notation of the East Anglians went not much further".

Mortal. Also used, like mort, as a superlative, as in "I am mortal hungry".

Mow. Gull, the bird, that is.

Muckweed. Fat hen (*Chenopodium album*), a member of the goosefoot family which is an abundant weed of cultivated land.

Nat-hills. Tussock sedge (*Carex paniculata*).

Needle rush. Hard rush (*Juncus inflexus*).

Needleweed. Shepherd's Needle (*Scandix pecten-veneris*), a native umbellifera growing on chalky soil.

Nettus. Neat-house, a building used for housing cattle. Neat is a very old word for cattle, and is still used by auctioneers who sell "neat cattle"; cf neatsfoot oil.

Norfolk plover. The stone curlew. It is not a member of the plover family, though in its feeding habits it does resemble them. It still breeds on the remaining brecks, but it has suffered much from afforestation and from intensive agriculture and is now considered a declining species needing special protection. The Rev Richard Lubbock wrote in the 1840s of its being abundant in the area between Thetford and Swaffham, where it might be seen in parties of 80 to 100 before migration.

Nutcrome. A stick, cut with a crook at the end to pull down the boughs when gathering nuts. See also **Crome**.

Oatflight. The chaff of oats, which is much lighter than that of other sorts of grain, was known as oatflight or sometimes just flights. It was once used by poor people for stuffing beds, or as Moor put it, "for the stuffing of bed picklin, or ticking, in the lack of feathers". Picklin or pickling was a coarse ticking used by seedsmen for making their seed bags, and by dairy maids for their aprons.

Off-hand. A farmer who has an outlying field or holding separate from the homestead is said to farm it off-hand. An Essex farmer who retired to the Suffolk village of Acton used to refer to his vegetable plot, on the other side of the road from his bungalow, as "Off-hand Farm".

Old sow, sowbug. The woodlouse, which when disturbed rolls itself up into a ball so that it is entirely protected by its carapace. "If swallowed in that state as pills, are believed to have much medicinal virtue in scrofulous cases, especially if they be gathered from the roots of aromatic pot-herbs, mint, marjoram, &c." says Forby. Moor merely observes that it was "sometimes swallowed as a cure for the ague".

Orphan John. Orpine (*Sedum telephium*), a native plant of frequent occurrence, also known as Livelong. It is said that Norfolk country people used to hang it up in their cottages, judging by its vigour of the health of some absent friend.

Ossel, norsel. A length of twine fitted to the head of a drift net, the upper end of which is fastened to the cork rope, allowing the net to hang about a foot below the cork rope. It might appear that the word was originally ossel, with the pronunciation norsel deriving from "an ossel", which carelessly pronounced becomes "a norsel"; but the *Oxford English Dictionary* spells the word nostel and gives a derivation from the Old English *nostle*.

Owl's crown. Wood cudweed (*Gnaphalium sylvaticum*), a native plant of heaths and woodland rides.

Pack-rag day. An old Suffolk name for Michaelmas Day, 29th September, "when servants remove with their bundles", as the Rev Sir John Cullum put it. Servants were usually hired at Michaelmas for the year, so for many it was a time of change.

Pagle, paigle. The cowslip. The same word is rendered as peggles in Essex. There is a Paigle Farm at Aldham, near Hadleigh in Suffolk.

Pail. Originally a wooden vessel for holding water or milk, but in more recent years made of galvanised iron sheet. In Norfolk the word is pronounced *paaile*. There is a story that when Caley's chocolate factory in Norwich was taken over by Mackintosh, a Yorkshire company, the Halifax-based production manager put up a notice at the Norwich factory stating that pails and cloths should be put in certain places, an instruction that was not always obeyed. The Norfolk workers said they did not understand the notice, as to them the articles were "paailes and dwiles"; some of the Halifax workers who had moved to Norwich also said they did not understand it, as in Yorkshire the articles in question were "buckets and clouts". Tiring of these excuses, the production manager put up new notices stating that "All pails, paailes, buckets, cloths, dwiles and clouts must be kept here".

Par-yard. An enclosed yard for cattle.

Pargeting. Ornamental plasterwork used to decorate many old houses in Suffolk and Essex. Outstanding examples are to be seen on the Sun Inn at Saffron Walden and on the Ancient House in the Buttermarket at Ipswich. The raised plasterwork is often painted in bright colours. Decorative plasterwork such as that on the Ancient House dates from the seventeenth century, but the word was used much earlier to indicate simply the covering of a wall with daub or plaster; from Old French *pargeter* or *parjeter*, to throw or cast over a surface (*par*, all over, plus *jeter*, to throw).

Parsley breakstone. The common saxifrage (*Saxifraga tridactylites*), a common native plant of dry banks and sandy places.

Peat cutting

Both in the Broads area and in the Fens the cutting of peat for fuel was a major industry, the broads themselves being formed by medieval turf cutting. Small-scale digging for peat continued on the Broads into this century, but in the Fenland peat-digging survived on a much larger scale in those areas that were not so effectively drained. Sybil Marshall has an excellent account of the trade in chapter three of *Fenland Chronicle*.

As with any other trade, there was a jargon that would be unintelligible to anyone unfamiliar with the work. A block of peat was a cess, the land to be dug was beatoned out using a line, and then the top layer of earth was pared with the hodding or paring spade. An area of land beside the piece to be dug was carefully prepared for laying out the cut blocks, and this was known as the staddle.

Each block, or cess, was $6^1/_2$ inches by $4^1/_2$ inches by $8^3/_4$ inches. Two courses were dug at a time, and if a pit was eight turves wide each row produced sixteen blocks, which was known as a slaughter. Fifteen slaughters would be dug to obtain two hundred, and eleven hundred made up a thousand, which in fact was 1320 cesses. If the pit were seven turves wide nine slaughters made one hundred, and ten hundred went to the thousand, that is, 1260 cesses. On average a thousand was approximately 1300 turves.

The variation in actual numbers is not surprising at a time when working men were not taught mathematics; they did, however, know how many slaughters they had to dig to obtain a thousand. Charles Lucas in *The Fenman's World* tells how the becket was introduced in Isleham Fen about 1856; it was a tool 14 inches long and $2^1/_2$ inches wide with an iron flange used for cutting the turves. A similar tool in Burwell Fen, however, was 18 inches long and 4 inches wide. The larger Burwell becket cut only sixty to the hundred; the rule in the trade was that if a hundred of Burwell turf was ordered, only sixty turves would be supplied.

As the turves were dug they were set off on to the staddle in rows three blocks wide and two high, these first two rows being the walls. Two more rows two blocks wide were set on top of the walls, these being known as the eccles. As the peat dried the piles of cesses were rearranged or dressed. There were several stages of dressing, known as edging, raising, turning and raffling. When the drying process was complete the turves were taken to the side of the nearest boat dyke for ricking; this entailed stacking them in ricks twenty-five blocks high.

Pass, in a. To be in a pass is to be thoroughly upset and annoyed about something. A correspondent in *Broad Norfolk* (1949) suggested it was a contraction of "in a passion," and contributed the example "Owd Mrs Harvey woos in some pass about har owd hins wot kep a-diein' orf one arter the tuther an' nobody dint know woi."

Peggles. See **Pagle.**

Penny-weed, Ha'pennies-and-pennies. Frogbit (*Hydrocharis morsus-ranae*).

Pickcheese. The blue tit. It is said that cheese was commonly used by boys for baiting the traps they used for catching tits.

Pickerel-weed. Water soldier (*Stratiotes aloides*), a once-prolific aquatic plant with stars of leaves resembling thistles. Changes in the Broads over the past 50 years have almost extinguished this plant, and efforts have been made by the Broads Authority to re-establish it in Barton Broad and other waters. Early attempts failed because the water quality was not sufficiently improved. Also used of the water plant *Pondeteria cordata*.

Major Moor mentions that pickerel weed was still well known in Suffolk and Cambridgeshire in his day—"and the idea that the sun's heat helps the breeding of pike in it is common", but one is uncertain to which of the two plants he refers.

Pickling, picklin. A coarse ticking used for seed bags and dairy maids' aprons. See also under **Oatflight**.

Pickpurse or sandweed. Corn spurrey (*Spergula arvensis*), a weed which grows commonly on acid soils.

Pighole. An apt description of an untidy room or of an uncared-for house.

Pightle. A small field or enclosure, sometimes formed at the junction of several larger fields. The word, of obscure origin, is not peculiar to East Anglia. Thomas Gardner in his *History of Dunwich* (1754) refers to a document of 1494 in which there is an item "My pytell lyinge in the Parische of All Seints within the said Town". The Barley Picle, a channel leading into the northern end of Yarmouth Roads, appears to be a phonetic variation of the same word. Forby's suggestion that it might be derived from the Italian word *piccolo* seems unlikely, but no better has come to hand. The Latin was *pictellum*, but that was probably a Latinization of the English.

A well-known and respected Norfolk businessman who named his house The Pightle was somewhat affronted one day to receive a letter erroneously addressed to him at The Pighole.

Pingle. Anyone who has mislaid his or her appetite is said to pingle the food. Moor

tellingly quotes a Suffolk man as saying "I hee'nt no stummach for my wittels. I jest pingle a bit."

Pinpatch. A winkle.

Pin-rush. Local name for the hard rush (*Juncus inflexus*) and sea rush (*Juncus maritimus*).

Pipe. A charge of powder or shot. Writing in the 1820s Major Moor says: "Some 30 or 40 years ago, the conveniences of patent powder-flasks and shot-belts, with suitable charges, were not much used among us; and we carried our powder in one bag, and our shot in another, with the bowl of a tobacco pipe in one or both." Although the pipe-

The long punt-gun held by Robert George Parker, of Rockland, in this photograph might well have taken "tew pipes of each."

bowl was no longer used as a measure at the time he compiled his *Suffolk Words and Phrases* the term pipe was still sometimes used, and he wrote of having heard it said of a long duck-gun that "she'll carry tew pipes of each".

Pitchfork. A long-handled fork with two slightly curved tines for pitching corn "in the straw" into waggons or, in relatively modern times, on to the stack. In the early nineteenth century, however, according to Moor, "Those who use it are called pitchers —those who unload the same into the stack or goof are called unpitchers". Forby also records the verb pitch, though one would have thought this not peculiar to East Anglia. In later days the pitcher was the elevator, worked either by a horse or later by a traction engine or tractor, used for raising the straw on to the stack during threshing.

Plancher. Forby, Major Moor and the Rev Walter Skeat all list plancher as a dialect word, but a glance at the *Oxford English Dictionary* shows that its use is, or at any rate was at one time, by no means confined to East Anglia. The dictionary does, however, quote Forby in one of its examples. The word is clearly from the Old French plancher. There is a lovely reference in the Paston Letters in 1449: "They ben scarse kne hey fro the plawncher". In some instances the word seems to have been used for an upper floor, but this might be merely an indication that in earlier times the ground floors were not boarded but of rammed earth.

Moor is somewhat more specific: he defines plancher as the floor of a bedroom, especially the part near the bed's foot.

The word is also used as a verb, meaning to cover a floor with boards. A building specification of 1516 from Cambridge reads, in part, "Also shall plancher all the chambers. . .with goode and abyl boorde of oak".

A specific East Anglian use of the word is for the covering board of a wherry, but it has been pointed out that this is no more than a mispronunciation of planksheer, the outermost deck plank covering the timber heads of the frames, otherwise known as the covering board.

Plash. To cut down a quick fence [a hedge] when grown old and stubby, and intertwine some of the lower branches, says Moor. He adds that it includes also the operation of overhauling the ditch and heightening the bank. Whether Forby considered it a word in general usage I do not know, but he omits it from his vocabulary; it is possibly one of those old words which survived in East Anglian dialect after becoming obsolete elsewhere. The origin of the word is to be found in Latin *plectia*, a twined or plaited hedge.

Moor quotes Thomas Tusser as advocating plashing in his February's husbandry:

Eat etch [stubble] ere ye plow—with hog
    sheep and cow.
Boy follow the plough—and harrow enough
    [obviously pronounced enow to rhyme with
    cow]
Sow pease not too thin—ere plough ye set in;
Late sown, sore noyeth—late ripe, hog
    stroyeth.
Cut vines and osier—plash hedge of
    enclosure.
Go strike off the nowls [the heads]—of
    delving mowls.
Too wet the land—let mowl-hill stand.
Trench meadow and redge [ridge]—dyke,
    quickset and hedge.
To plots not full—add bramble and hull
    [holly].

Plumpendicular. Not really a dialect word, rather a confusion of plumb-line and perpendicular, yet it is a delightful expression. "But, however good and valuable the word may be, it is in danger of perishing when village carpenters shall attend, as a part of their education, a course of lectures at a Mechanic's Institution," says Forby. An article in the *Evening Star* in 1972 concerning the Suffolk dialect was headed "Thet might be dyin, but thet in't dead". Long may it survive.

Plural

In common with modern Dutch, the East Anglian dialect does not use the plural form in expressions such as "I walked ten mile" and "two pound of tea".

Poker. The reedmace, either lesser or great; a typically descriptive dialect word for a plant whose head reminds one of the poker used to stir up a fire.

Pokers or Redheads. Norfolk name for pochard, a duck which has been extending its range in recent years, and is a winter visitor to the broads.

Pollard, or powled tree. A tree which has had its head, or poll, cut off so that new branches grow from the top of the stem or tod. Moor attributed the popularity of pollarding in Suffolk—"this barbarous custom," he called it—to the fact that the loppings or stowins were the tenant's perquisites, whereas a timber tree belonged to the landlord. There is, however, another reason: the roots of trees planted alongside marsh or fenland roads helped to protect the road edge, but if the tree were allowed to grow to its full height it would easily be blown down in a storm; pollarding not only produced a good crop of useful poles every few years but reduced windage and encouraged the tree to produce a good root system.

Pollywiggle. A term used in Suffolk, and elsewhere, for the tadpole. Sir Thomas Browne, the Norwich doctor-naturalist, noted in 1646 that "the spawne is white, contracting by degrees a blacknesse, answerable. . .unto the porwigle, that is, that animal which first proceedeth from it". Forby refers to polliwigs or purwiggy, and traces its origin to periwig, though he observes that "one of the little animals bears as much resemblance to that antiquated article of finery, the wig with

a long queue, as to a pot-ladle, by which name we also call it". Well, in 1529 a "perwyke" was made for the King's fool; but the word polwygle in the sense of a "wyrme" had appeared about 1440, some years before the peruke seems to have made its mark on the English fashion scene.

Poor outs. "We made poor outs on't" means simply that someone did badly.

Pot-ladles. A Norfolk name for tadpoles, derived from their shape. According to Spurdens another name used for the little tadpole was dish-ladle.

Power of, a. A large number, quantity or amount of something, another instance of a once-ordinary word that has survived only in dialect. Fuller's *Worthies*, published in 1661, refers to "a power of poor people" being employed in processing pilchards. As a child, one was told that a particularly nasty medicine would "do you a power o' good", and later on one heard of people who had made "a power of money" from some scheme or other.

Progue, to. To poke or probe, a word still used in parts of Suffolk.

Puckaterry. Being in a proper puckaterry is, in ordinary English, being thoroughly upset. The word is almost certainly a mispronunciation of purgatory, but the sense in which it is used is entirely local to East Anglia. Several correspondents in *Broad Norfolk* (1949) mentioned the word, and in spite of one remarking that his spelling was "entirely phonetic" they all used the same spelling.

Pudden, pudding. A toad. Pudding Moor, the roadway in Beccles running at the foot of the cliff along the edge of the marsh, is said to have gained its name from the toads found there.

Puddenpoke, oven tit or ovenbuilder. The willow tit, from its beautifully constructed nest, or the long-tailed tit. These names are also used for the chiffchaff. Moor adds an explanation which, though he thought it superfluous, will no doubt be appreciated by today's readers:

"I crave to be allowed one line of lamentation over the article so unmeritedly discarded, the Pudding Poke, which I hope the reader requires not to be told was a long taper bag, in which that esteemed edible was boiled of yore—and much better boiled than it can be in the round form of the present fashion. By the time that the centre of a round pudding 'is enough', the circumference is boiled to insipidity. We may regret the departure of the days when the pudding, of ample longitude, was turned out into the savoury browned 'latch-pan'; and, garnished with hard dumplings, came smoking to table as the first dish! The expressive old saying 'You must eat another yard of pudden first,' i.e. before you be man enough to do so and so, will soon be obsolete, and unintelligible." Which, of course, it now is.

For those who wonder at his mention of the latch-pan, he explains this as the dripping pan with the gravy or "drippen" of the roast meat "latching" in it.

Puit. A Norfolk name for a black-headed gull or Scoulton cob.

Pulk or pulkhole. In Norfolk, a small pool or marsh pond, or an inlet among the reedbeds on the margin of a river or broad. In Suffolk, a small pond used for domestic water supply to a nearby dwelling.

Push. A boil. Another of those words which seems to have come to us from the Dutch

Pronunciation

The local pronunciation is now, at the end of the twentieth century, fast disappearing. There was a time, less than fifty years ago, when the village in which Sidney Grapes kept a garage was known to all as "Po'er Ham", though spelt Potter Heigham. Not only is the "T" now sounded in the first element but the second is pronounced "Hayham"; it is probably only a matter of time before the area outside the Norwich city walls to the west, known as Heigham, changes from "Ham" to "Hayham".

Many words are pronounced by the East Anglian speaker in a manner quite different from the Standard English. Major Moor, returning after lengthy service in India, remarked on the way Suffolk men turned "boots" into "butes", "fool" into "fule".

Thus "cool" becomes "cule" and "cooler" becomes "culer", the familiar and much-used word "do" is pronounced as "dew", the children go off "tew skule" and return home in the "arternune".

Yet there are other words written with a double-O that are not pronounced in this way. A broom is generally a "brum", and the roof of a house is a "ruff". Vowels are also changed in a number of other words, with "sheep" being shortened to "ship" in Suffolk; the Shipwash Sand off the Suffolk coast has wrecked many a fine vessel, but the name is derived from the appearance of the waves breaking in the shallow water which from the shore look like the fleecy backs of a flock of sheep.

and Low German; in modern Dutch a pimple is a puist. It had entered the English language by the early sixteenth century, however, so it could be one of those words once in general use that have survived only in the dialect.

Pyewipe. The lapwing or peewit.

Quackled. Choked or suffocated, see **Cackle**.

Quant. A long pole bearing a turned wooden "bott" at one end and an iron-shod toe, together with a wooden foot to prevent it sinking into the mud, at the other. It is employed to propel a wherry, a reed lighter or other boat in shallow waters, in a calm or

against the wind when tacking is impossible because of the narrowness of the waterway. It was also used to give a wherry a set off from the bank, either to assist her in going about or to enable her to creep along the lee shore. A full-size wherry's quant used to be 22 feet long, but this was increased to 24 feet when the Norwich River was dredged to a greater depth; handling so large a quant required considerable skill and stamina. Yacht quants are much smaller.

Queech, squeech. An untilled, rough bushy corner of a field, according to Major Moor. There is also a suggestion of a wet place. This is a once-common word that has survived only in the dialect; it is recorded as far back as the fifteenth century. See also **Spong**.

One of the wherries seen at Yarmouth in this photograph by Payne Jennings is being quanted by a member of the crew, who has to walk on the overhanging cargo of deals.

A ransacker setting up a drift net in a Lowestoft net store.

Quicks. Couch grass or twitch (*Agropyron repens*), a pestilential, creeping weed of cultivated land and the bane of gardeners.

Quill. A wooden pipe made up of four boards fastened with iron plates for carrying water through or under a river. Quills feature in the Ipswich town records, where the word is used for water pipes used in the town supply. The dry dock at Flatford, portrayed in John Constable's painting "Boat-building on the Stour", has a quill passing under the river to empty the dock into the delph ditch on the far side.

Rafflejack. The corncrake, a bird which began to decline towards the end of the nineteenth century and now appears in East Anglia only as a migrant on passage. The dialect name is descriptive of its grating call.

Rafty. Cold and damp, as in "rafty old weather" or "a rafty morning". It has been suggested that the word originated in the late eighteenth or early nineteenth century when Napoleon was threatening to invade England with an army carried on rafts, but this ingenious explanation of the word fails when one finds it in use in the mid-seventeenth century. Its real origin is obscure.

Ranny. A shrew. The most abundant and widespread of the shrews is the common shrew, *Sorex araneus*; how come that the latin name has become its common dialect name, or is it the other way round?

Ransack, To. To search for something that is missing, originally in a legal sense to search a house or person for stolen goods. From the Old Norse *rannsaka*, to seek.

Ransacker. An employee in a net store who was responsible for inspecting nets as they came into the store to assess the amount of damage requiring repair. In the better days of the herring fishery many nets were repaired by outworkers who beat the nets either at their back door or in a garden shed, and it was necessary to estimate the amount of work to be done. In later days the ransacker set the net up after the beatsters had completed their work, fastening the norsels to the cork rope.

Rattle-basket. Yellow rattle (*Rhinanthus minor*), a marsh plant whose seeds rattle in the pods as the wind blows.

Ratweed. The name used in the Broads for lesser duckweed (*Lemna minor*).

Redweed. Corn poppy (*Papaver rhoeas*), which can be an abundant weed in sandy areas of arable land.

Reed pheasant. Broadland name for the bearded reedling (*Panurus biarmicus*) or bearded tit. This distinctive bird of the reedbeds belongs to the babblers (*Timaliidae*) and not to the tit family. In the nineteenth century the activities of gunners and collectors brought this little bird to the brink of extinction, and in 1898 it was estimated that no more than thirty-three pairs had nested successfully in the whole of Norfolk. The Rev Richard Lubbock, who most strangely omitted this bird from his *Observations on the Fauna of Norfolk*, asked a marshman to shoot some bearded tits for him "for preservation" but regretted that when he received them they had been almost blown to pieces by the large shot used; he supplied the marshman with dust shot, and later received six birds killed with one shot. The bearded tit became a protected species in 1895 and has at times greatly increased its numbers, but it is extremely vulnerable in prolonged periods of hard winter weather.

Reek. Used in West Suffolk of what is called elsewhere a clamp, of potatoes, mangels or other root crops.

Reign. To continue in use, said of a ship or boat. Edward FitzGerald notes it among his Sea Words, quoting "The Hebe was an old ship ten year ago; but she reign still, I hare." Daniel Defoe uses the word of Ipswich colliers in his *Tour Through the Whole Country of Great Britain* (1724): "They built also there [Ipswich] so prodigious strong, that it was an ordinary thing for an Ipswich collier, if no disaster happened to him, to reign (as the seamen call it) forty and fifty years and more."

Roaring. The action of turning over a heap of herrings to mix in the salt used as a preservative, using a wooden roaring shovel not unlike the maltster's shovel. The word appears to be derived from the Middle Dutch *roeren*; in modern Dutch the verb *roeren* means to mix. A basket used for transporting the salted herring was known as a roarer.

Rocket. A portion of work. See **Droppen**.

Rodges-blast, Roger. A whirlwind which occurs in the area of the Broads. Forby gives: **"Roger's-Blast**, s. a sudden and local motion of the air, no otherwise perceptible but by its whirling up the dust on a dry road in perfectly calm weather, somewhat in the manner of a water-spout. It is reckoned a sign of approaching rain." There is here a suggestion that the word was then of general East Anglian usage, but today it is most often heard in the Broads region.

Christopher Davies has something to say of the **"rodges-blast"** in *Norfolk Broads and Rivers* (1883). "It is really a rotary wind-squall or whirlwind, and is most likely to occur with

Fish market workers with their roaring shovels.

a south-west wind. Sometimes the blasts are very violent, and come without warning. Even if you see one coming over the marsh, convulsing the grasses or lifting the reed-stacks high in the air, you cannot tell whether it will strike you or not, its course is so erratic. It may wreck a windmill fifty yards away, and leave the water around you unruffled. It may blow the sail of one wherry to pieces, and another wherry close by will be becalmed. Occasionally you may see a dozen wherries in the same reach, all bound the same way, with their sails now jibing, now close-hauled, now full and now shaking, with the fitfulness of the wind. Sometimes, in a large reed-bed, you may see the reeds all laid flat in a circle, or in a carr the trees uprooted for a space, where a rodges-blast has descended. Now and then, although rarely, a veritable waterspout crosses the country, and does great damage when it breaks."

Sometimes the word is associated with Roger Bigod, one of William the Conqueror's henchmen whose descendants became Earls of Norfolk in the twelfth century.

The spelling varies considerably, with several of the correspondents whose letters were reprinted in *Broad Norfolk* in 1893 referring to this phenomenon as a **Sir Roger**. One of them refers to a tradition that the name was derived from "the unquiet spirit of Sir Roger Ascham", but it was of much earlier origin. About 1440 John Lydgate wrote that

> I haue herd seid of ful yore agon
> A whirl wynd blowing nothing soft
> Was in old Englissh callid a Rodion,
> That reiseth duste & strauh ful hih alofte.

The pronunciation of the word is made plain by the alternative spelling Rodjon.

Walter Rye

It would have been surprising if Walter Rye, the Norwich solicitor-antiquary, had not involved himself in dialect study. The English Dialect Society published his *Glossary of Words used in East Anglia founded on that of Forby, with numerous corrections and additions* in 1895.

Rye was well aware of the pitfalls into which the dialect researcher could tumble. "I cannot help thinking that many of the words included in the following pages are only the imperfect remembrance by an ignorant countryman of some 'good word' which took his fancy," he wrote. "Only two or three years ago, being in the company of a little farmer who was extremely fond of using long and fine words, I remember mischievously asking him whether he did not think it fine 'feasible' weather for his crops, and he jumped at the word, and soon after I heard him repeat it to a friend.

"*Pea-goosin*, 'prying about like a peahen'; *cabobble*, 'to confuse'; *squackled*, *sploddin*, *quavery-mavery*, *ruffatory*, *hammer-snouting*, *rumgumptious*, *undercumstumble*, *rumbustical*, *dardledum due*, and others, are words framed after the fashion of Lewis Carroll, and in most cases are omitted from these pages, as they are not dialect at all. One might as well insert such words as *tootsicums*, *babsicums*, *coodlicums*, and *popsy wopsy*."

He was also aware of the need not to take himself too seriously, and told several stories in his preface of the kind that the *East Anglian Magazine* of the 1950s included in its "East Anglian Humour" pages. Tales like the one about the youngster who cried out "Look, there's some red blackberries!" "Ye fule," said his companion, "they're allus red when they're green." One hopes present-day readers will not require the explanation that Walter Rye thought necessary for his Victorian readers!

Rodges-blast or Sir Roger, the name is derived from a word of unknown origin that in the fifteenth century was spelt rodion or rodjon.

Rond. The swampy margin of a river or broad between the water's edge and the river wall. A word derived possibly from Old Norse but found also in Dutch and German, meaning a bank or border. In some parts of the country the same word was used for the skirts of a field. The Dutch word *rand*, meaning a rim or ridge of hills, has found its way into Witwatersrand, the elevated ridge in the south Transvaal which forms the barrier between the Vaal river and the Olifants river; the Rand became famous for its gold mines.

Rond-stuff. Rond-grass (*Glyceria maxima*).

Round the bend. Deranged, insane. See **Doolally**.

Rowens. Feed left on meadows or grasslands after being mown. See **Aftermath**.

Sacking billy. Farmworkers and others seeking to protect themselves against the weather would take an old sack, cut arm holes and a hole for the head, and slip it on over their other clothes. This was known as a sacking billy.

Saddlebacks. A descriptive term for the Black-backed gull, both the Great (*Larus marinus*) and the Lesser (*Larus fuscus*). The Great Black-backed came to East Anglia in their tens of thousands for the Autumn or Home Fishing, and B.B. Riviere in *A History of the Birds of Norfolk* (1930) gives an evocative account of the birds' involvement in the herring fishery: "On the drifters the majority of the nets are hauled about dawn, and one may say that practically all are hauled between 2 am and noon, the process taking from four to eight hours, according to the size of the catch, and longer in bad weather.

After hauling, the whole length of nets are shaken over the side and cleaned as the boats steam back to Yarmouth harbour. During the whole time the nets are being hauled, even at night, but in far larger numbers after daylight, the great Black-backs are flying round the boats, picking up the herrings which fall out of the nets and the broken fish which are thrown overboard, and even seizing the fish out of the nets themselves, and each boat as she steams homewards is followed by a cloud of Gulls constantly stooping down to the water to pick up the fish which are shaken out of the net in the process of cleaning."

Sammodithee. An expression of great antiquity, if one is to believe Forby, who found it mentioned by Sir Thomas Browne, the seventeenth-century philosopher and physician. Another philologist, referred to by Forby in his long and learned note, interpreted it as "Say me how dost thou", pointing to the Saxon "saeg me hu dest thu". The derivation of the expression turned out to be more down to earth than the antiquaries and philologists expected.

Spurdens came upon the real meaning of the expression by accident. "The first time I ever heard it, or of it, was from Mr W. Hooker, now Sir W.H., who breakfasted with Mr Deere and myself, at his cottage at Brundall. He was just come from Mr D. Turner's at Yarmouth, where he also had first heard of it, and inquired if we knew anything about it. A day or two after Mr D. and I went to visit the site of St Benet's Abbey; and, sitting on the staging of the mill upon the ancient gate there, I poured out two glasses of ale, one of which I took for myself, and handed the other to the well-known Peter Pike, of South Walsham, who had conveyed us thither in his boat. 'A health to you, Peter,' said I. 'Sammodithee,' replied he.

"An explanation ensued; and the result was that the cabalistic expression was not a mode of salutation, but a reply to one; and being interpreted, was merely, 'Same unto

A Victorian gathering at St Benet's Abbey, where the Rev William Spurdens came upon the real meaning of Sammodithee when handing Peter Pike a glass of ale.

thee.' Amid the bogs and fens, which surround the old Abbey's mouldering fragments, we had ample opportunity, before the day was closed, of testing the matter. 'Good evening,' said to a ploughman on his way home from labour or to a boatman gliding past us on the river, brought out, more frequently than any other expression, the mysterious 'Sammodithee, sir!'"

Scissor-grinder. Grasshopper warbler, whose voice has been described as a high-pitched trilling similar to the winding of a fishing reel—or the sound of a scissor-grinder's treadle grindstone, perhaps.

Scoulton cobs. Blackheaded gulls, which established one of their gulleries on Scoulton Mere in the Breckland long ago. It was referred to by Sir Thomas Browne in the seventeenth century. At one time the gulls' eggs were collected, and in 1860 no fewer than 15,000 eggs were gathered in this colony.

Scutcher. A metal scoop used on board drifters to transfer herring into a basket. It has been suggested that as the scoops had rather the shape of a shield the word is derived from the heraldic escutcheon, itself derived from the Latin *scutum*, a shield.

Erwarton Church.

Sea-pie. The oyster catcher.

Sea-plodder. An old term used on the Suffolk coast for a porpoise.

Seal, sel. Time or season, as in Haysel, hay-making time, Barleysel, the time of sowing barley, and Barksel, the season of stripping bark from the oaks for tanning. A country-man will give his neighbour "the seal o' the day" as they pass in the road.

Seft. The past participle of to save. "I were a'goin through the stuff in my drawer, 'n' I seft this for you."

Sele. Use of the word is well illustrated in a brass in Erwarton Church to Phillipe Parker, who had died in infancy, which bears the epitaph:

> A short accompt a reconing very small
> The Seely Soule shall at his dooming find
> when he his race a yere and more had run

Though some "furriners" like to refer to Silly

Erwarton Church, which contains a brass referring to "The Seely Soule." The first element of the name is, by the way, pronounced like the er *in clerk; indeed, the name used to be spelt Arwarton.*

Suffolk the correct word is sele, not silly. It means holy.

Serpent's tongue. Arrowhead (*Sagittaria sagittifolia*), a water weed which grows in some of the marsh drains and in the upper reaches of some of the Broadland rivers.

Shannocks. A name for the inhabitants of the Norfolk coastal town of Sheringham, many of whom voyaged far afield in search of crabs in their double-ended fishing boats, to which the same name was transferred in course of time. Some Shannocks settled in the Lincolnshire port of Great Grimsby after that town had become the terminus of the Manchester, Sheffield and Lincolnshire Rail-way and had begun to develop as a fishing port, their boats being a familiar sight in the lock pit at the entrance to the docks. It is said that at one time the entire crew of the Grimsby lifeboat was made up of Sheringham men. Others settled at Hornsea, on the Lincolnshire coast, and at Whitstable in Kent, among other places. There is no obvious reason why the Shannocks were so keen to move away from Norfolk while the inhabitants of the nearby town of Cromer apparently were not.

Shanny. One who is shanny is out of his mind, but to shinny-shanny is to play the fool.

Sheep's parsley. A Suffolk name for what is known elsewhere as cow parsley (*Anthriscus*

sylvestris). One of the earliest forms of vegetation to grow under the hedgerows in spring, it would be eagerly devoured by sheep being driven down the road to fresh fields and meadows.

She-gladdon. The greater reed-mace (*Typha latifolia*).

Shepherd's Sundial. The scarlet pimpernel (*Anagallis arvensis*).

She-reed, soft reed. The reed canary-grass (*Phalaris arundinacea*) and also second-growth reed (*Phragmites communis*), which lacks the flowering plumes and is inferior in terms of quality for thatching.

Sheres, the. Any county in England outside Norfolk, Suffolk and Essex. Forby remarks that this appears to be the ancient pronunciation of shire. A **shere-man** is, he says, "any

A group of Sheringham fishermen or Shannocks photographed about the turn of the century, no doubt discussing some item of local "politics."

man who had not the good fortune to be born in one of the sister counties, or in Essex".

Shim. A white mark on a horse's forehead, otherwise known as a blaze. The word comes from Old English *scima*, brightness or splendour.

Shimmer. A heavy haul of herring. The word might possibly be derived from the silvery appearance of the herring as the net is hauled.

Shoe-awl. The avocet. The dialect name is presumably a reference to the bird's up-turned beak.

Shoeing the cowt. "Any person in a parochial or other office who attends a public meeting for the first time, is called a 'colt' (pronounced *cowt*), and must be 'shod;' that is, must pay a forfeit in liquor for the benefit of the company," says Forby. Maybe so, but the custom had its origin in the harvest field, where any young man who had not previously taken a harvest would be known as a colt and would be expected to pay for a gallon of beer. Any who proved unwilling to provide beer would be seized and up-ended so that the older men could hammer at the soles of his boots until he acquiesced.

Shove. Not specifically a dialect word, but rather an instance of a word in general English usage that is derived from a Scandinavian source. In Norway hotel doors bear the word *skjov* (pronounced shove), meaning *push.*

Shroud. "I h'int never sin a shroud with a pocket" is a familiar Suffolk way of saying that a man cannot take his money with him.

Shruff. Fragments of sticks, bits of coal, cinders, etc. picked up by the poor for fuel, says Forby, who spells it *shrough*, while point-ing out that it is pronounced *shruff.* The word was used of small hedge trimmings, *shruff-stuff* as Moor calls it, which was at one time claimed by the hedgers as their perquisite. In Suffolk a **shruff hut** was a temporary shelter for farm equipment with horizontal beams supported by uprights of rough timber in the round; brushwood was piled on the horizontal beams and thatch laid over it.

Shutting-in time. Sunset; the time at which the animals were shut up for the night.

Shy. Used, in contradiction to the usual meaning, of a boy or girl whose conduct was considered wild and unsteady. A shy boy or a shy girl, says Spurdens, was wanton, unsteady or amorous, and in his editing of Spurdens' supplement to Forby the Rev Walter Skeat adds a note that "At Acle, for instance, a shy girl is a bold girl, one wanting in bash-fulness".

Sight of, a. A great number, as in "What a sight of people there are here, to be sure!"

Silly bold. Impertinent, rude. A boisterous child who is becoming too wild would be told, "Now, don't be silly bold". This expression has not yet disappeared from use in Suffolk.

Sir Roger. See **Rodges-blast**.

Skink, to. To serve at table, says Forby, particularly to serve the guests with drink. A **skinker** is one who serves drink. "In alehouse parties, in which the word is principally used, it is applied to one of the company who takes upon himself to fill the glasses or horns, and to call for more liquor, when it is wanted. The waiter, who brings it in, is not called the *skinker*, but the *tender.*" A tender, he explains, is a waiter at a public table or at a place of entertainment. Again we have a word of Dutch origin, from *schenke*, remembering that in Dutch the *sch* is given a hard, indeed guttural, pronunciation.

Explaining *tender*, Forby tells an amusing story of having heard the word "uttered with great force, and a true East Anglian accent, from a box in Vauxhall Gardens. On passing near it, not without some apprehension of being recognised by his countryman, he was more fully convinced of his being so, by hearing him address a pretty blushing young woman of his party as 'Peg Maa'r'."

The word tend is no longer used of waiting on company at table, but it is still used of looking after cattle and other animals.

Skransh. "The act of chewing or munching any thing that sounds short under the tooth, green apples, raw carrots, hard biscuits," says Moor.

Skuppit. A shovel with parallel sides which are turned upward and even a little inward, and a T-handle. Moor also mentions a

A shuppit at the Museum of East Anglian Life at Stowmarket.

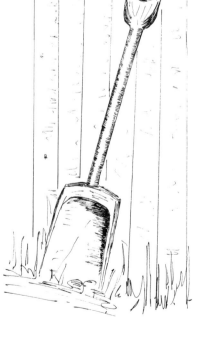

skaffel (or **skavel**), which he describes as a small skuppet used in draining "and in out-hawling or feying narrow bottomed ditches". Both words are used by Thomas Tusser, who farmed in Suffolk.

Slads. Muddy ground from which the water has receded, or pools of floodwater on the marshes.

Slub. Alluvial ooze, particularly the soft mud that gathers in the bottom of a dyke as a result of silting and the decay of aquatic vegetation. Possibly adopted from the Dutch (in modern Dutch *slobber* is sludge or slush), it is a word of some antiquity; John Norden (1548–1625), who was in 1593 "authorised and appointed by her Majesty to travil (sic) through England and Wales to make more perfect descriptions, charts and maps", referred in his *Speculum Britanniae* to land which "fortefies it selfe with heaped mountes of sande, slub and pibble-stones".

Major Moor remarks that "wet, poachy ground, recently trodden by cattle, is said to be slubby, or all of a slub", and adds that "walls raised from the ooze of rivers require to be slubb'd over, that is, the interstitial chinks or fissures caused by evaporation, require to be filled up with more of the slub, or alluvial deposit".

Slubbing out. The operation of removing slub from a dyke or drainage ditch. It might be done with a mud-scuppit, a shovel or scoop sometimes made of wood. See **Skuppit**.

Sluff. A wooden scoop used in the Fens, much the same as the mud-scuppit referred to above.

Smartweed. Pale persicaria (*polygonum lapathifolium*), a weed of arable land.

Soft rush, soft water-rush. The blunt-flowered or fen rush (*Juncus subnodulosus*), a common plant of the mowing marshes.

Sole, to. To beat, in the sense of "give a good hiding". Many a mother has been heard to say to her truculent offspring, "I'll sole you if you speak to me like that!"

Sorrel. Chestnut coloured; or when referring to a Suffolk horse, chesnut. The Sorrel Horse is, as the Raynbird brothers put it, "not an uncommon sign for an alehouse," though many of these old hostelries have closed down since their day. Sorrel was the name of the horse that put its foot in a molehill and threw Dutch William, leading those with Jacobite sympathies to toast "the little gentleman in black velvet".

Sosh, on the. This expression, meaning that something is out of perpendicular, is not used universally throughout East Anglia but is known in Norwich and in a number of other places both in Norfolk and Suffolk. More usual is "on the huh".

Sowbug. The woodlouse. See also **Old sow**.

Speet. Wooden rods with one pointed end on which fish were hung to cure in the smokehouse. The word *speet* is no more than a variant pronunciation of *spit*, a cooking implement used in the kitchen. Sprat speets were thin pieces of split wood; herring speets were much larger, about five-eighths inch in diameter and four feet long. While herring speets were used for smoking bloaters **baulks** were used for kippers; these were rectangular pieces of wood about four feet long with hooked nails driven in along each side on which the split herring were hooked.

Spiflicated. Surprised, astonished, stammed. "A low quaint word," says Moor, who includes it in his *Suffolk Words and Phrases* of 1823, thus proving that the word is of some antiquity in spite of its sounding like a humorous fabrication. In fact it was recorded in the eighteenth century, and is not specifically East Anglian.

Spile. A stout wedge of wood tipped with iron and used in clay or gravel pits to let down large quantities of material at once. This operation was known as **caving**. A word that has come to us from Dutch, it is also used for a pile for such work as supporting an embankment. "It is likewise our pronunciation of *spoil*," adds Moor to his definition of the word.

Spile, spile-peg. A small wooden peg driven into the spile-hole or air hole of a cask; it has to be loosened or removed when the contents are to be run off. More than one hostelry that once rejoiced in a traditional name such as the Lamb or the Sorrel Horse now has the sign of the Tap and Spile, but few who drink within appreciate just what a spile is.

Spink. The chaffinch, the name being derived from the bird's call note. The goldfinch is sometimes called the **goldspink**.

Spong. The Rev Sir John Cullum says simply a narrow slip of land, and Forby adds "such as a strong active fellow might clear in a *spang* or leap". Moor is more explicit, describing it as "an irregular, narrow, projecting part of a field, whether planted or in grass. If planted, or running to underwood, it would be called a squeech or queech. Spinny is another indefinite word applied like dangle, reed, shaw &c. to irregular bushy plots or pieces of land". See also **Queech**.

Spoonbeak. The shoveller, a duck that feeds by filtering its food off the surface of the water.

Spoon-puddens. Otherwise called drop-dumplings—"both are good names of a good thing," says Major Moor appreciatively. They were made by simply dropping spoonfuls of batter, with or without currants, into boiling water. See also **Swimmer**.

James Spillings and "Giles's Trip to London"

One writer who used dialect to excellent effect in his comic books was James Spillings (1825–1897), who is today remembered chiefly for the delightful little books in dialect published by Jarrold & Sons, which sold in their thousands during the latter part of the nineteenth century and for some years into the twentieth.

The first, *Giles's Trip to London*, first appeared with a note addressed to the editor of the *Eastern Daily Press* dated August, 1871: "Mr. Giles Hobbins, who is just returned from a visit to London, has sent for me to write out the story of his adventures. He says he wants the people of these parts to know all about it. He is a good honest fellow, and you may rely on the truthfulness of his tale."

397TH THOUSAND.

"GILES'S TRIP" SERIES.

PRICE SIXPENCE EACH
GILES'S TRIP TO LONDON.
MOLLY MIGGS'S TRIP TO THE SEASIDE.
JOHNNY'S JAUNT.
JACK JAWKINS'S FIRST VOTE.
THE COCKNEYS IN THE COUNTRY.
PRICE TWOPENCE.
'ARRY AND 'ARRIETT AT YARMOUTH.

JARROLD & SONS, 3, PATERNOSTER BUILDINGS, LONDON.
And London and Exchange Streets, Norwich.

It seems that after the tale first appeared in the *Eastern Daily Press* it was amended to make it "interesting to dwellers in Suffolk and Essex" and published in the *Ipswich and Colchester Times*, a paper which had a relatively short life. It must have been the latter improved version that was taken up by Jarrold & Sons for wider circulation.

Born in Ipswich, James Spilling became an apprentice in the printing office of the *Suffolk Chronicle* and as a young man founded the Ipswich Utilitarian Society, an organisation of which little is remembered. He was an active member of the Chartist movement and a preacher at the Swedenborgian New Jerusalem Chapel in Ipswich. In 1863 he moved to Norwich, where he presumably joined the congregation of the Catholic Apostolic Church meeting in St. Mary-the-Less in Queen Street.

The success of *Giles's Trip to London: A Farm Labourer's First Peep at the World* persuaded Spillings to write further humorous tales such as *Johnny's Jaunt: A Day in the Life of a Suffolk Couple*, *Molly Miggs's Trip to the Seaside: A Country Woman's First Peep at the World*, *The Cockneys in the Country: A Diverting Story, in which the tables are turned on the Londoners*, *Johnny and Jenny: Their Wonderings and Wanderings on their Way to Lowestoft* and *'Arry & 'Arriett at Yarmouth: A Tale about Norfolk Dumplings*. Copies of these inconsequential little books occasionally appear in second-hand bookshops, and *Giles's Trip to London* has recently been reprinted, but *Giles and the Grand Old Man: A Norfolk Labourer's Views on Mr. Gladstone's Visit to East Anglia* is rarely seen these days.

Sprank. A flaw, crack or split in a rail or other piece of wood. According to Moor, in this condition it was said to be spranked. Cf **Sprunk**.

Sprunk. A broken mesh in a drift net. If two meshes were broken, it was a **crow's-foot**. Cf **Sprank**.

Squit. A diminutive or insignificant person, or as Forby put it, "a word of supreme contempt for a very diminutive person". The origin of the word is obscure, but Forby points to the Old English *squib*; "but that word seems to be lost, and the more is the pity, for at any rate it was less offensively contemptuous," he adds. Another word for a contemptible fellow is a squinny, according to Spurdens.

Squit. Nonsense, stupid or silly talk. It seems likely that this meaning is a development from the last, for the word is not noted in this sense by Moor, Forby or Spurdens. The earliest written evidence of this usage is given by Cozens-Hardy in *Broad Norfolk*, a little book of letters reprinted from the *Eastern Daily Press* in 1893: "Some people may look upon this correspondence as a lot of

A circular saw in operation at the Little Welnetham rake factory, which closed in the 1980s. Scythe stailes were made here in a large jig which imparted the necessary double bend.

squit and slaver (nonsense), but they need not look as sour as wadges about it," he wrote. Today the word is well known in Norfolk and Suffolk; "Thass a lot o' ol' squit" is the dismissive comment on many an official statement from government bodies.

Staile or stale. A handle, especially of a scythe, or the rung of a ladder. The word is a very old one indeed, one of those that survived only in dialect; it is still to be found in Flemish. In the fifteenth century one finds the word *stele* used of the handle of a pan or other utensil. The curved staile of a scythe was often shaped by being fitted into a jig; the staile of a rake, on the other hand, was made of the straightest available piece of wood. At the end of the nineteenth century there were half a dozen rakemakers in Suffolk, who would doubtless also have produced scythe stailes, and in this century there was a rake and handle factory at Little Welnetham, Suffolk (with a showroom in

London), whose machinery appeared to have been designed by Heath Robinson.

Staithe. A quay, wharf or landing stage. The word, which is by no means confined to East Anglian dialect, appears to be derived from an Old Norse term for a landing stage; it is found wherever Viking influence was strong, and on the Tyne is used specifically for the quays at which coal was loaded from the collieries. In North Norfolk it has entered the placenames, in Burnham Overy Staithe and Brancaster Staithe; on the Broads almost every riverside town and village had its staithe, sometimes owned by the parish but sometimes by private landowners, a difference that has in several cases led to conflict and law suits. At King's Lynn the Common Staithe was originally owned by the Trinity Guild, but by the charter of 1548 the Corporation acquired possession not only of the staithe but of other property belonging to the guild.

Stammed. Amazed, taken by surprise. A man might say he was "wholly stam'd" by some unexpected turn of events.

Stank. A wooden dam put across a stream or dyke to stop the flow of water.

Star-grass, starch-grass. The bog-rush (*Schoenus nigricans*), a common plant of mowing marshes.

Staunch. Pronounced staanch. A device found on the Little Ouse and on some Fenland navigations similar to the flash locks found on other early waterways, designed to hold back the water to enable vessels to navigate the river. It had a gate that could be raised vertically by means of a large hand-wheel at one side. When the gate was raised a flash of water ran through the gap, and barges or lighters bound downriver could be taken through on the flash; those bound upriver had to be hauled through against the current. Cf. **Stank.**

Stetch. The ploughed portion of land between two furrows, greater or less according to the heavy or light quality of the soil, state William and Hugh Raynbird in their book *On the Agriculture of Suffolk*, published in 1849. "In strong land we go eight furrows to a stetch, called eight-furrow work," they say, quoting Major Moor.

Stick-'n-a-half. A flail. The handle, usually made of ash, is the handstaff or staile, the swingel is the part that swings; that was usually of blackthorn or some similarly tough wood. The joint might take several forms, but typically it consisted of a strip of green ash cleverly shaped to form a looped cap known as a capple on the end of the

A staunch on the Little Ouse at Brandon, one of five which enabled lighters to reach Thetford.

handstaff; a piece of ox-hide or an eelskin threaded through the loop was fastened to the swingle to provide a simple hinge.

Stifler. An official, a person in some position of minor authority. In the sixteenth century the word seems to have been *stickler*. The head man or farm foreman was often known as the hid stifler, the word "hid" being the Suffolk pronunciation of head.

Stive. A dialect word for dust, as in "don't sweep so hard with that there broom o' yours, you're raising a dreadful stive". Forby indicates that in the nineteenth century at least it could be used as a verb, giving as an example "Go gently, Tom, you stive the ladies," said to an awkward fellow who kicks up clouds of dust in riding or walking. It is just another of the many words that have come from the Dutch; the *Oxford English Dictionary* gives its derivation from the Dutch word *stuive*, related to *stuiven*, to raise as dust, and records that the word seems originally to have belonged to Pembrokeshire, where there was a Flemish colony, and to East Anglia, where words from the Dutch are frequent.

Stockerbait, stocker. Unwanted fish, or fish of an unwanted variety, that was considered the perquisite of the crew; or the money received from the sale of such fish, which was divided among the crew. Cf stockfish, the wind-dried cod imported from Iceland in the Middle Ages.

Stonerunner. The dotterel.

Story teller. One who does not stick too closely to the truth.

Stover, stuvver. Winter food for cattle, particularly clover made into hay. Major Moor comments that "we rarely confound a 'hay-stack' and a 'stack of stuvva', the latter appearing to be confined to clover; or extended sometimes to sanfoin and other artificial grasses." Tusser makes use of the term many times, and there are other sixteenth-century examples. The word also used to be employed more generally as food, either for persons or for animals, for a journey. J.J. Hissey in his *Tour in a phaeton through the Eastern counties* (1889) remarked on the notice he saw at Woodbridge, "Stover sold here". The forms stuvver and stuvva (which is how Major Moor spells it) are nothing more than the East Anglian pronunciation of stover. The *Oxford English Dictionary* traces the word stover to estovers, from the Old French *estovoir*, to be necessary; estovers meant wood or other material which a tenant was privileged to take from his landlord's estate so far as it was necessary for repairing his house, hedges or implements.

Stovey. What is known elsewhere as stoved potatoes is stovey in parts of East Anglia. It is a dish in which potatoes predominate, with an onion, pepper and salt; a cheap but filling one to which can be added anything that comes to hand.

Straff, straft. Anger, a scolding bout. Sir Thomas Browne knew the word in the seventeenth century, J. Steele listed it about 1712, and Forby included it in his vocabulary. It is therefore surprising to find the *Oxford English Dictionary* describing the word *strafe* as slang, "From the German phrase *Gott strafe England*, 'God punish England', a common salutation in Germany in 1914 and the following years". The earliest example there given is dated 1916, but from East Anglia some much earlier examples might surely have been found, albeit verbal ones. The origin of our word is fairly evident from the above.

Streeking board. A Suffolk term for an ironing board. Originally it was "that on which they stretch out and compose the Limbs of a dead Body", but in course of time it came to be merely the board on which the linen was stretched out. To streek was to iron clothes. The word seems to be from the Old English *streccan*, to stretch, and was also rendered *strike*.

Stuggy. A word meaning stocky, thick-set. The word was much used in East Anglia, but it is clear that it was also used in other dialects including Devonshire. The origin of the word is unknown, but there are indications that it might be found in Dutch.

Suckling. White clover (*Trifolia repens*), a grassland weed that also grows on newly made paths and on the roadside.

Summerland, summerlay. Land left without a crop for one year; it was ploughed five times, and then crab-harrowed four times to eradicate the weeds. That was no good in a dry time, though, because the weeds did not chit. Bastard summerland was land sown

Swills on the Fish Wharf at Yarmouth about 1903.

with a clover mixture, cut once and then ploughed; normally the clover would produce a second crop and be harvested for seed.

Summer snipe. The green sandpiper.

Swill. A basket of peculiar form made of unpeeled willow, used only at Yarmouth for landing herrings; a wicker handle nipped the swill into almost a figure-of-eight shape. Manufacture of swills long predated the introduction in 1908 of the cran measure; a swill held two-thirds of a cran of herring. In 1879 there were a dozen basketmakers in Yarmouth, all of whom would have made swills. The last man to make them, up to the 1950s, was a member of the Bird family. The origin of the word is unknown, but its use for a fish basket goes back at least to the fourteenth century.

Swimmer. A Norfolk dumpling. If badly made so that it was soggy and heavy instead of light and fluffy, it was a sinker. A cook aboard a Lowestoft drifter, a boy of thirteen or fourteen, found at his first attempt that the dumplings were indeed sinkers; "don't throw those dumplings overboard," he was told, "they might damage some ship's propeller!"

Swipe, swape, swike or swake. The handle of a pump. In the case of the wherry's wooden-cased pump the word was used for the pump itself, which is not surprising when one finds that around 1700 a swipe was "an Engine to draw up Water". It is a word of Anglo-Saxon origin.

Teamer-man. A team-man, one who had charge of a team of horses, "a post of dignity and ambition", as the Rev W.T. Spurdens says in his supplement to Forby.

Teens. Just to show that there is nothing new under the sun, Spurdens, writing in 1840, includes in his supplement to Forby "Teens, the years of life between twelve and twenty", and as an example quotes a youngster as saying "In a month I shall be into my teens."

Teeter-ma-tawter. Descriptive dialect word for a seesaw. The word has been written teeter-cum-torter, but Eric Fowler, "Jonathan Mardle" of the *Eastern Daily Press*, expressed the view that this was probably the invention of some parson or schoolmaster who wrote Norfolk but did not speak it; he was almost certainly correct in that view. The expression "on the teeter" has been used of something that is tilted. In America a seesaw is well known as a teeter or teeterboard, but the East Anglian has added somewhat to the original form of the word. Originally **titter-toter**, the word is a very old one; in 1530 it was "Tytter totter, a play for chyldre".

Tenchweed. The broad-leaved pondweed (*Potamogeton natans*), a plant with bronze-tinted floating leaves found in quiet bays around the broads and in the deeper Broadland dykes.

Thack, twig-rush. The great saw-sedge (*Cladium mariscus*), which can dominate the fen and have a strong influence on the natural development of a Broadland landscape.

Thead. A part of the impedimenta of brewing, the tall wicker strainer placed in the mash tub over the hole in the bottom to ensure that the wort runs off clear. "It is perhaps more commonly called a *fead*," says Forby, adding "No unusual change." It is probably not exclusively East Anglian, as it appears in the *Oxford English Dictionary*, but as Forby's definition is quoted therein, it has been admitted.

Throstle. A song thrust.

Thrower. A knife with the handle at right angles to the blade used for cleaving lath and hurdle stuff. "It appears to have been formerly called frower," says Moor, giving us a good clue to its origin. A frower or froe is a cleaving or riving tool of some antiquity; Thomas Tusser lists among the tools needed by a husbandman

> A grindstone, a whetstone, a hatchet and bill,
> A frower of iron for cleaving of lath.

Thunderstone, thunder pipe. A belemnite, or a similar small stone of cylindrical form. "We fancy some of them fall in thunder storms," says Moor, "and I am not sure that we are altogether in error. The persuasion— I had written superstition, but crossed it out—is old and perhaps extensive."

Tidy. This word is used in two senses, meaning either cleanly and neat or as a superlative. A tidy body is an active, cleanly person, "a good recommendation to a servant," as the Rev Sir John Cullum said. "A good tidy bit" or "a good tidy crop" would mean a largish piece or a bountiful crop. Thomas Tusser, who farmed at Brantham, used the word:

> If weather be fair, and if tidy thy grain,
> Make speedily carriage, for fear of a rain;
> For tempests and showers deceiveth a many,
> And lingering lubbers lose many a penny.

Something that is done well is done good tidily; a lesser man might do it half-tidily.

Tightly. Promptly, actively, alertly, says Forby, quoting from Shakespeare's *The Merry Wives of Windsor*: "Hold Sirha, beare you these Letters tightly".

Ting, to. To ring a small bell or **ting-tang**, to summon the family to dinner, the congregation to prayers, etc. Forby explains further that "To ting bees" was to collect them together when they swarm "by the ancient music of the warming-pan and the key of the kitchen-door; the melody of which is still believed to be very efficacious".

Titlark. The meadow pipit.

Titties, tits. Teats, says Forby, "the very Saxon word, *titte*".

Tittle, to. To tickle.

Tittle-my-fancy. The pansy (*Viola tricola*).

Titty, titty-totty. Very small. From Scandinavian; in Norwegian dialect *titta* is used for a little girl.

Tizzack. A persistent rasping cough. One who was suffering from such a cough might say "I fare a bit tizzacky".

Toadskep. A Norfolk word for a fungus, literally a toad-basket, quoted by the Rev Greville J. Chester in 1857.

Tod. The stump of a tree. The word is also used of the trunk of a pollarded tree, one which has had its head (*poll*) cut off so that new branches shoot from the top.

Together. A word frequently used in East Anglia (often rendered "togithers" in Suffolk), not always in a collective sense. A

A forge at Kirby-le-Soken, in the Tendring Hundred, with the blacksmith's name over the travus.

young lady, staying for the first time with her young man's family, was covered in confusion when she came down to breakfast in the farm kitchen and was asked "Did you sleep well, togither?"

Togs. Small crabs.

Tom tit. In Suffolk this is a blue tit, but in other parts of East Anglia the name refers to the great tit.

Trave. A wooden frame in which an unruly animal could be restrained when being shod. Until just a few years ago there was a trave in the yard of a veterinary surgeon's premises in Bungay, and there is still one outside the disused forge at Belstead, near

Ipswich. Chaucer knew the word: in the Miller's Tale he describes Alisoun, a high-spirited young lady:

And she sprong as a colt doth in the trave.

Travus. The section of a blacksmith's forge in which the horses were shod. It has been taken to be a version of traverse, the partition dividing the travus from the forge itself, but George Ewart Evans has shown that it is in fact the trav'us, the house in which the trave was kept.

Triculate. To adorn or decorate; to finish something off. The normal word in common English usage is titivate, which the dictionary defines as "To make small alterations or additions to one's toilet, etc., so as to add to one's attractions; to make smart or spruce; to 'touch up' in the way of adornment, put the finishing touches to." One

A tumbler, a two-wheel cart that was made to tip and thus discharge its load.

might suppose the East Anglian word to be a mere mispronunciation of titivate, but the earliest example of the use of titivate given in the OED is only from the early nineteenth century, while Forby in 1830 seems to regard triculate as a well-established word; perhaps triculate is the older word. Forby adds that "It is used by masons, for putting the last hand to what they mean to be smart and shewy."

Trinkum-Trankums. Odd pieces of finery such as trinkets, ribbons and so on. This word is mentioned only by Spurdens in his supplement to Forby, but it is a delightful and very descriptive compound typical of those dialect words which gave the local speech such richness.

Trolly. A market cart, says Major Moor, meaning a light four-wheeled vehicle with a flat bed. At Yarmouth the trolly, or troll-cart, also called a harry-carry, was a two-wheeled vehicle with the wheels set inside the frame specially developed in the town for negotiating the narrow rows; it was found nowhere else.

Truck. Rubbish, as in "thass not no good a' all, thass just a load o' ol' truck".

Trunk-way. A culvert carrying the water of a ditch under the approach to a gateway. In general usage it is a boxlike passage, usually made of wooden boards, for passing air, light or water, but in Norfolk and Suffolk it was used to refer to an arch of brick or masonry as above. Forby remarks that the name doubtless arose from the use of hollowed tree trunks for the same purpose "in ancient and simpler times, and even now [1830] in the few woody parts of both counties". See also **whelm**.

Tumbler. A tumbril or two-wheeled farm cart. It might be thought that this is no more than a mispronunciation of tumbril, a word said to be of Old French origin, but Forby points out that the name is exactly descriptive. "A tumbler is made open behind, and occasionally closed by a tail-board. . .On the removal of this, and a strong wooden bar before, which, passing through two iron hold-fasts, secures the body to the shafts, the carriage tumbles backward and discharges the load." Indeed, the word tumbler seems to have as good an ancestry as tumbril, for it is found in seventeenth-century writings. The tumbler was in due course largely superseded by the Scotch cart, made in quantity by firms like Woods of Stowmarket and Smyths of Peasenhall, the latter better known for their seed drills.

Tunnel. A funnel, a device for pouring liquid into a small aperture. Forby commented that this word was in constant use in his time, and was a much better word than funnel, which had been substituted for it. Certainly the word was in use in the sixteenth century, and was retained in East Anglian dialect at least until the nineteenth.

Turnpike sailor. A tramp.

Tussock. A clump of matted grasses or other vegetation, particularly of the tussock sedge (*Carex paniculata*), which has played a significant part in the growing up of the broads. It eventually forms huge, close-set stools as much as three or four feet high and begins to crowd out reeds and other aquatic vegetation. Such tussocks were sometimes cut and trimmed to provide rough seating in cottages or hassocks for churches, as Forby describes: "These hassocks in bogs were formerly taken up with a part of the soil, matted together with roots, shaped, trimmed, and dressed, a sufficient part of their shaggy and tufted surface being left, to make kneeling much easier than on the pavement of the church, or the bare boarded floor of a pew."

Tuttle. A scythe-like implement with a short blade used by marshmen to cut underwater plants.

Tuttle box. A piece of wood sometimes suspended between a pair of horses drawing a plough, says William Waters in *Norfolk Archaeology*, 1879. It sometimes had a sharp point on one side, the object being to prevent the horse walking on the unploughed land from "crowding" against the horse in the furrow.

Twizzle, to. To turn a thing round and round between the fingers, quickly and repeatedly, says Forby. He also quotes an example of a more general sense in which it was used, "He came *twizzling* down"—and this is quoted in the *Oxford English Dictionary*, which describes the word as an imitative formation suggested by *twist*. Almost certainly not peculiarly East Anglian.

Tye. A common, an area of open ground on which those who have common rights may graze their animals. The word, which has come down to us from Old English, is confined to part of Suffolk (Barking Tye, for example) and to north Essex.

Under-butter. The butter made of the second skimmings of milk in the dairy districts of Suffolk. It was never sent to market but was either kept for domestic use or sold to near neighbours for prompt use, as its keeping qualities were poor.

Undernean. Underneath, in the precise sense that not only is one thing below another, but that at the same time it is near it, says Forby. It comes from the Old English *underneoðan*; there is an Old Danish equivalent, *underneden*.

Ungain, ongain. An adjective meaning inconvenient, unpromising or unprofitable, derived from the Old Norse *ugagn*. Forby gives as an example "The land lies ungain for me." As early as the fifteenth century we have "The lady seyde, We ryde ylle, thes gates they are ungayne".

Up-a-day. A fondling expression of a nurse to a child, when she takes it up in her arms, or lifts it over some obstacle, says Forby, who suggests a derivation from the Anglo-Saxon *upadan*. The modern version is *upsadaisy*.

Upland. "Higher and drier ground, as contradistinguished from fen-land," says Forby. One of the outlying hamlets of the parish of Kersey in Suffolk is known as Kersey Upland; though it has no great elevation, it lies out of the valley that shelters the main settlement. An **Uplander** or **Uplandman** is an inhabitant of the uplands. In the Fens the preoccupation with height is even more noticeable; Shippea Hill has no elevation at all but is one of the gravel patches that just broke the surface when the area was flooded.

Upstart, startup. The deep impression made by a horse's hoof in clay soil. Forby explains how the impression soon filled up with water, which, when another horse happens to tread in the very same place, starts upwards and plentifully bespatters the rider.

"These up-starts, or start-ups, as they were otherwise called, were a great nuisance some forty years ago in the rich district called High Suffolk, in which it was then almost impossible to travel otherwise than on horse-back; though now [about 1820] it is easily and commodiously passable by carriages of every kind, on good roads," the good parson adds.

Vacagees. The accusation is often made that dialect is nothing more than slovenly speech, and it has to be said that the rendering of some modern words by countrymen lends support to this quite erroneous supposition. When children were evacuated from London at the beginning of the Second World War those who were temporarily settled in East Anglia were called by many people *vacagees*. It was soon realised that because of its geographical position and the number of RAF aerodromes in the region East Anglia was not a safe place for children, and they were moved elsewhere, to be followed by considerable numbers of East Anglian youngsters. Another widely used modern dialect word is *nocolate* for pollinate, presumably an abbreviation of inoculate.

Van. A flat basket used for winnowing corn, also called a **Fan**. It was used to throw the threshed corn into the air, allowing the wind to remove the chaff. From Old English *fann*.

Viper's Dance. St Vitus's Dance, an illness of which one of the symptoms is extreme trembling. Probably no more than a confusion with the original.

Virgin Mary thistle. Major Moor records that this name, presumably dating from pre-Reformation days, was given to the blessed thistle (*Carduus benedictus*), whose broad leaves are marked with well-defined white spots, as if they had held milk. He sets down the legend that Our Lady, when thirsty, met with a cow; and having no vessel for receiving the milk, used the broad leaf of the thistle as a cup. This beautiful thistle has ever since retained the marks of the milk. This legend is not, he says, confined to Suffolk.

Wain. A heavy four-wheeled vehicle for the carriage of goods, from Old English. The word *waggon* came into use in English only in the sixteenth century from Dutch and German, apparently having been learnt by men fighting in the continental wars. John Constable's famous painting of Flatford is entitled "The haywain".

Wakes. Patches of clear water on an otherwise frozen broad.

Walks. Forby defines a walk as an unenclosed cornfield, and correctly suggests that the word is derived from the sheep-walks of the Middle Ages. "As this right is extinguished in all Inclosure Acts, the name is in danger of perishing," he says; yet today the Ordnance Map still bears the names of several walks in the area between Westleton and Blythburgh, and Toby's Walks is a popular picnic site set out by a benevolent district council beside the A12 just south of Blythburgh.

Wall, to lie by the. One who lies by the wall is dead. It was, says the Rev Sir John Cullum, of Hawsted, spoken of a person between the time of his death and burial.

Water-bewitched. "Very weak grog; or poor tipple in general," explains Moor. In other words, drink that has been too much diluted. No doubt it would also be used of milk that had been watered down; a farmer guilty of adulterating his milk was said to have "the cow with the iron tail", a reference to the pump from which his "milk" had come.

A Norfolk marsh seen in one of P.H. Emerson's photographs. Such marshland was often waterslain.

Wattle and daub construction seen in an old house in Lavenham.

Waterslain. Land which retained surface water was thus described.

Wattle and daub. A means of infilling the frame of a timber-framed building. Hazel branches were nailed across the timbers and tied with brambles, then well-puddled clay was daubed by hand on the branches or wattle and smoothed down. A coat of lime plaster would then be skimmed over the face of the clay wall, and this would be lime-washed. The wattles could be nailed across the face of the timbers to provide a draught-proof wall, or alternatively they could be fitted between the timbers in order to leave the timbering exposed.

Wennel. A weaned calf.

What for. A youngster will be promised "what for" by his mother if he does not behave himself. If he fails to do as he is told he will probably find that "what for" is a thrashing (or a *troshen*) when his father comes home from work.

Whelm. Half a hollow tree laid under a gateway to carry the water of a ditch. "A bad substitute for a brick arch," says the Rev Sir John Cullum in his list of words in use at Hawsted in the eighteenth century. See also **trunk-way**.

Whitsuntide flower. The guelder-rose (*Viburnum opulus*).

Wholly, hully. Entirely, completely, used in the sense of a superlative, as in "He wholly riled me, doin' what he did," or "That were that funny, I wholly laughed at that."

Wild vine. White or red bryony (*Bryonia dioica*), a common native plant of hedges, scrubland and woods.

Willow-weed. The great hairy willowherb (*Epilopium hirsutum*) and amphibious bistort (*Polygonum amphibium*).

Wind-egg. An egg without a shell, or with a very thin shell.

Windhover. The kestrel, which hovers while keeping an eye out for movement on the ground. Significantly, perhaps, the Dutch name for the kestrel is *windhaver*.

Windle. A winnowing fan or basket. It is not recorded by Forby or Moor, but it is in William Waters' list of 1879. It is apparently derived from the Old English *windwian*, winnow. The word is also used for a basket to hold corn or other material, in which case the origin is Old English *windel*, from *windan*, to plait. As late as the 1950s the word was still used at Yarmouth of baskets employed to coal steamships; these windles were carried along planks from the quay to the ship, and were said to hold about 12 stone of coal each.

Winterweed. Ivy-leaved speedwell (*Veronica hederifolia*).

Woodcock owl. The short-eared owl, which as a passage migrant arrives in East Anglia about the same time as the woodcock.

Wooden hill. The staircase. "Come on, less git up the wooden hill te bed."

Woodwose. A wild man figure which became a popular feature of church decoration in the fourteenth and fifteenth centuries, though he was almost certainly pagan in origin. As portrayed on a number of fonts in East Anglian churches the woodwose is a wild man, covered in hair and carrying a hefty club, but the green man of roof bosses and similar carvings is usually a head intertwined with foliage, often with the foliage issuing from the mouth or sometimes from the sides of the face. It is possible that these carvings are derived from the May Day rites, in which Jack i' the Green is a man entirely hidden by a wicker frame decorated with leaves and other greenery. The Green Man as a pub sign is often now seen as a Robin Hood figure, but in time past he was synonymous with a wild man; there is a Wild Man at Sproughton and another in the centre of Norwich.

Wretweed or wartweed. Sun spurge (*Euphorbia helioscopa*), a common weed in cultivated land, whose juice was said to produce warts.

Wrong. A term used for a crooked timber, usually a tree bough, much sought after by shipbuilders to form the curved timbers and knees. It is a word which has come to us from the Old Norse *wrange*, bent or curved. A very similar word is still used in Norwegian and Swedish for a ship's ribs.

Yarmouth capon. Major Moor tells us that this was a name for a red herring, a hard-cured salted herring of the kind exported in large numbers to the Mediterranean in sailing vessels in the nineteenth century.

Yawl. Pronounced *yoll*, derived from the same root as the Dutch and Danish *jolle* and the Swedish *julle*. A type of open sailing boat used off the Norfolk and Suffolk beaches by the beach companies during the nineteenth century for putting pilots aboard vessels, for attending upon shipping lying in Yarmouth and Lowestoft Roads, for salvage work and sometimes for lifesaving. Until the 1840s these boats were rigged with three masts, each with a lugsail, though it was usual to leave the mainmast ashore in severe weather and to use only the foresail and mizzen; from about 1853 a two-masted rig was adopted, with a dipping lug foresail and standing lug mizzen, the *Mosquito* belonging to the Young Company of Lowestoft being the first two-masted yawl.

Largest of all the yawls was the 74-foot *Reindeer*, built by Jermyn and Mack at

World-wide travels of a dialect

There is a common belief that the decay of the English language and the decline of dialect began in the 1930s when the Hollywood talkies introduced American slang into Britain. What is not generally realised is that much American English usage is in fact an archaic form of the language which has been superseded on this side of the Atlantic—*gotten* was a form commonly used in England up to the eighteenth century, and the spelling *harbor* is found in literary use in this country in the same period—and that colloquial American English shows signs of having absorbed many features of our East Anglian dialect.

In one of the early Westerns the cowboy gallops into town and breathlessly asks, "Say, bo', where's the sheriff?" Bo' is in this case not a variant of *boy* but a derivative of the Old English *gebur*, meaning a friend or mate; just the same, in fact, as the East Anglian *bor*. The Westerner might comment on the speed of a horse, "That hoss is going some fast!" In doing so he not only uses the typical East Anglian pronunciation *hoss* but also employs the word *some* in a peculiar way in place of *very*; this usage is shared by East Anglian and American speech.

It would seem, therefore, that some of the "slang" introduced by the movies was actually making a return journey. A small American-British dictionary published in the 1970s includes the word *bum*, meaning a tramp, and comments that "this is one of those words from America that has now established more than a toe-hold in Britain and will probably be widely accepted soon with this meaning, rather than the anatomical one." As a term of personal opprobrium *bum* dates back in English usage at least to the sixteenth century, so its acceptance represents a comeback rather than a new introduction.

Even that peculiarly American word *cute* was known in ordinary English long before it returned with American servicemen in the Second World War, as was pointed out by John Greaves Nall as long ago as 1866; "a very common Americanism, of East Anglian origin," he observed. It was used in eighteenth-century English to describe someone shrewd, sharp and quick in apprehension.

Nall listed upwards of fifty words and expressions in common use both in East Anglia and in America, though in some cases the exact meaning had changed after export. Even the word *furriner* as applied to those not fortunate enough to have been born in East Anglia was, he said, to be found in use in the Southern States of America, where *foreigner* was used to describe those born in another state. Perhaps it was not only the usage of the word that was exported but the attitude that led to its being so used.

It need not surprise us that East Anglian dialect has been assimilated into the common speech of the Southern States and of New England, for a great many of the early settlers in America came from Norfolk, Suffolk and Essex. Eighteen years before the voyage of the Pilgrim Fathers, a Suffolk man, Bartholomew Gosnold, explored the coast of New England and discovered Cape Cod, so named by him because of the abundance of codfish in the vicinity. Later he took part in the expeditions to Virginia which also involved other East Anglians, including John Smith, known as "the father of Virginia", and John Rolfe of Heacham, who married the Indian "princess" Pocahontas.

About a dozen of those who went out to New England in 1620 in the Mayflower—a Harwich ship with a Harwich captain, for all that she cleared from this country at Plymouth—were from the three eastern counties, and they were followed out ten years later by more than 150 men, women and children from Suffolk and nearly another hundred from Essex in the Winthrop Fleet, led by John Winthrop of Groton, who became the first Governor of Massachusetts. Governor Winthrop's son John established the town of Ipswich, Massachusetts, in 1633 and later became Governor of Connecticut.

Those were the pioneers; they were followed by many more emigrants from Eastern England in the years that followed. They, too, played their part in establishing the regional dialect on that far-off shore.

The Rev Edward Gepp investigated the links between the dialect he recorded in the Essex parishes of High Easter, Felsted and Little Dunmow and the common speech of the United States and came to the conclusion that the negro talk of Georgia and Virginia represented English speech of the sixteenth and seventeenth centuries. Much of his evidence he found in *Uncle Remus* and other books by Joel Chandler Harris. The thought of Brer Rabbit, Brer Fox and the rest talking in Essex or Suffolk dialect might seem ludicrous, but just consider the phrase "got down on laugh fit ter kill hisse'f;" is that not near as can be to the East Anglian idiom?

The African workers adopted the speech of their masters, some of whom undoubtedly came from our region of England. "It may be that the negro unconsciously adopted our eastern talk as the easiest, rejecting the difficult dialects of the north and west," Gepp wrote. "But, whatever the reason, the fact remains that in the present dialect of these States our east country words are as thick as the plums in a reasonably rich plum-pudding."

The theme was taken up by George Ewart Evans in 1957 in a series of articles in the *East Anglian Daily Times* in which he points to other parallels between East Anglian and American dialects. He, too, searched American folk-tales, legends and ballads, and quotes an instance: "Brer Bear he has acres en acres of good bottom land: Brer Rabbit he des 'ev a small sandy-land farm." Bottom-land and sandy-land were once common terms in Suffolk, one indicating heavy, low-lying land often serving as meadows and the other the light land now generally referred to as the Sandlings.

"A study of some of the modern American writers from the South appears to show that not only has the speech affinities with the dialect of Suffolk but that particular customs and usages point fairly conclusively to a common origin," says Ewart Evans.

As if to drive the point home, he cites a speech by John Bright, the advocate of free trade, at Rochdale in 1863 in which he told of the experience of a Suffolk country gentleman visiting the United States: "When he stepped from the steamer on to the quay at New York he found that 'everybody spoke Suffolk'."

Yarmouth in 1838 for Denny and Brock's company, headed by Joseph Denny and Samuel Brock, the latter being the most famous of the beachmen. With Brock at the helm the *Reindeer* was very successful in the local regattas, and in 1851 when the schooner yacht *America* won the Queen's Cup at Cowes the beachmen issued a challenge to sail the *Reindeer* against the yacht for a stake of £200. It is said that the owner of the *America*, John Stevens, sent a friend to Yarmouth to investigate; having seen the speed of the yawl on a reach the friend advised Stevens to decline the challenge on the grounds that the *Reindeer* was an open boat, not a yacht. Instead of declining the challenge Stevens raised the stakes to £1,000, a sum which the beachmen had no hope of raising. The beachmen felt that in a sense they had won the challenge, since in their opinion the *America's* owner had resorted to trickery to avoid the risk of defeat.

With changing circumstances the yawls went out of use. The last to be built for salvage work was the *Sophia*, for the Kessingland beachmen about 1911 and broken up for firewood in 1933; it is likely that the last yawl to be used in service was the *Eclat* at Caister, last launched in 1919. Many were sold to pleasure boat proprietors at places like Southend and Clacton-on-Sea for use as trip boats; one which was sold to a King's Lynn fisherman was partly decked in, rigged like the other Wash fishing craft as a cutter, and became the prototype of a type pro-duced by local boatbuilders known, not unnaturally, as a yawl.

Yelk, yulk, to. To level and ram clay in forming a floor, or to knead clay with straw or stubble in preparation for the daubers. See **Wattle and daub**.

Yelm. A tight, compact layer of wetted straw ready for thatching. A word of Anglo-Saxon origin with similar forms in Dutch and other languages, it is not strictly an East Anglian term. In Old English it had a more general meaning of a handful or sheaf of corn.

Yelm, to. To prepare the yealms for thatching. Edward Turner describes the operation in his book *Memories of a Gamekeeper's Son* (1997):

> I had to stand sideways on and bend low to pull the straw from the bottom of the "bed", the heap of long straw that had been wetted and left overnight to help straighten the straw. You drew from the bottom because the weight of the straw above would allow the wet straw to pull out straight.
>
> As you pulled the stalks out you shuffled them forward in front of your legs, and laid them evenly. You worked from one end of the bed to the other, pulling out double handfuls of straw and laying them side by side. When you reached the end of the bed, the resulting quantity of straw was a yealm. Seven yealms were tied to a handle, what we called a yoke, and you then had a "bunch" ready for carrying on to the stack for the thatcher to use.

Fareyewell, moind how ye goo!

Bibliography

C. Benham. *Essex Ballads.* Colchester, 1895 and subsequent editions. New edition illustrated by Andrew Dodds, Colchester, 1960.

Broad Norfolk, Reprinted from the Eastern Daily Press. Norwich, 1893. Edited by H.T. Cozens-Hardy.

Broad Norfolk, written by the Readers of the Eastern Daily Press, Jan. 21st–March 19th, 1949. With an introduction by "Jonathan Mardle" (Eric Fowler). Norwich, 1949.

G.J. Chester. "Norfolk Words not in Forby's Vocabulary," in *Norfolk Archaeology,* vol V, pp 188–192, 1857.

J.B. Clare. "A Glossary of Old Fashioned Words." In *Wenhaston and Bulcamp, Suffolk.* Halesworth, 1903.

A.O.D. Claxton. *The Suffolk Dialect of the Twentieth Century.* Norman Adlard, Ipswich, 1954.

Cullum, Sir John. "Some words and expressions used in this place [Hawsted] and the neighbourhood." In his *History and antiquities of Hawsted,* 1784.

E. FitzGerald. "Sea Words and Phrases along the Suffolk Coast," in *The East Anglian, or Notes and Queries,* Vol III, pp. 347–363, 1869.

R. Forby. *The Vocabulary of East Anglia; An attempt to record the vulgar tongue of the twin sister counties, Norfolk and Suffolk, as it existed in the last Twenty Years of the Eighteenth Century, and still exists; with proof of its antiquity from etymology and authority.* 2 vols, London, 1830. Reprinted, Newton Abbot, 1970.

E. Gepp. *A Contribution to an Essex Dialect Dictionary.* George Routledge, London, 1920. 2nd edn, 1923.

S. Grapes. *The Boy John; A selection from the Boy John's letters to the Eastern Daily Press in Norfolk Dialect, 1946–1958.* Norwich, n.d.

S. Grapes. *The Boy John Again; A second collection of the Boy John's letters in Norfolk dialect to the Eastern Daily Press.* Norwich, n.d.

"Jonathan Mardle" (Eric Fowler). *Broad Norfolk.* Wensum Books, Norwich, 1973.

E. Moor. *Suffolk Words and Phrases; or, An attempt to collect the lingual localisms of that county.* Woodbridge and London, 1823. Reprinted, Newton Abbot, 1970.

J.G. Nall. *An Etymological and Comparative Glossary of the Dialect and Provincialisms of East Anglia, with Illustrations derived from native Authors.* Part II of *Chapters on the East Anglian Coast.* London, 1866.

W. & H. Raynbird. "Local words in use among the labouring classes." In *On the Agriculture of Suffolk*, London, 1849.

W. Rye. *A Glossary of Words Used In East Anglia founded on that of Forby*. Oxford University Press for the English Dialect Society, London, 1895.

W.W. Skeat, ed. "East Anglian Words; from Spurdens' Supplement to Forby, 1840." English Dialect Society, *Reprinted Glossaries*, Series B, XX, London, 1879.

W.W. Skeat, ed. "Words in Use at Hawsted, Suffolk; from The History and Antiquities of Hawsted and Hardwick, in the County of Suffolk, by the Rev Sir John Cullum, Bart. F.R.S. and F.S.A., second edition, London, 1813." English Dialect Society, *Reprinted Glossaries*, Series B, XXI, London, 1879.

K. Skipper. *Larn Yarself Norfolk*. Nostalgia Publications, 1997.

B. Slaughter. *Let's Git Up Agin the Table. A social history of diet and cooking in the Essex and East Anglian region largely from the words of those who did the growing, the cooking and the eating.* Essex Federation of the Workers' Educational Association, Colchester, 1992.

B. Slaughter. *An Essex and Suffolk Alphabet*. Published by the author, n.d.

P. Trudgill. *The Dialects of England*. Basil Blackwell, Oxford, 1990.

P. Trudgill. *The social differentiation of English in Norwich*. Cambridge University Press, 1974.

C. Upton and J.D.A. Widdowson. *An Atlas of English Dialects*. Oxford University Press, 1996.

W.G. Waters. "Norfolk Words not found in Forby's Vocabulary," in *Norfolk Archaeology*, vol VIII, pp167–174, 1879.

D. Woodward. *Larn Yarself Silly Suffolk*. Nostalgia Publications, 1998.

F.B. Zincke. *Some Materials for the History of Wherstead*. Ipswich, 1887.